Cold Machine

COLD MACHINE

J.R. VERLIN

Orbis Tertius Press

Alberta, Canada

Cold Machine © 2023 J.R. Verlin

Cover design and interior layout by Kimberley Palsat

Original cover photograph from the series "Naked vs. Nude," debuted at Downtown Los Angeles' The Hive Gallery.
"With Eyes Locked" by Johnny Cubert White (2013)
#myBROKENcamera
@johnnyCUBERT

ISBN: 978-1-7781566-3-2

"He who makes a beast of himself gets rid of the pain of being a man."
- Samuel Johnson

ONE

It happened one afternoon in the San Fernando Valley: eighty-five degrees and blue skies. February might be a wintry month in some places, but here in the land of endless summer, the changing of the seasons was almost meaningless.

I coasted through the suburb of Porter Ranch on my mountain bike. Northwest valley—horse country—the asphalt so smooth I could ride without handlebars. Luxury vehicles gleamed in driveways of hand-laid brick and cobblestone. Lawns vivid green, every border and walkway edged with precision, saltwater pools and grottos dug into the backyards. I pulled into a Mediterranean-style home roofed in red tiles; an ornate fountain babbled in the front courtyard. Resting my bike under a climbing Bougainvillea I fixed my hair, smoothed my white dress shirt, and straightened my black tie. I slung my backpack off my shoulders and reached in to grab my Bible and the accompanying LDS pamphlets. Leaving the bag behind, I walked to the arched doorway while mentally rehearsing my speech. After a deep breath, I rang the bell.

A blurry shape appeared through the opaque glazing, softening into something more delicate as it formed. The door opened. On the other side was a young woman in a silk bathrobe, bouncing blonde hair and cherry lips. Bare feet on terra-cotta floors.

Our eyes locked, she smiled. "Yes?"

My mouth was dry, voice nowhere to be found.

She giggled, waving her hand. *"Hello."*

I snapped out of it. "Hi, hello, good afternoon," I said. "My name is Logan Pierce and I'm an elder from The Church of Jesus Christ of Latter-Day Saints."

"Ohh," she said, her eyes scanning me from top to bottom. "A Mormon boy." She extended her hand. "Please, call me Wendy. Wendy Waves."

"Pleasure to meet you," I said, reaching out.

"Impressive grip," she said. "You must be very good with your hands, Logan."

"I, uh, thank you, Wendy," I said, yanking back. "By chance, is your husband home?"

"My husband?" she said. "I'm twenty-two years old. I have ambition. I'm not a simple housewife."

"I'm sorry, I didn't mean—"

"But you're right," she said, cutting me off. Then, with a sly grin, "I don't live here alone. This is my *Daddy's* house. And no, he isn't home. He's away on business." She fingered the lapel of her robe. "It's just me here, bored and all alone."

A bead of sweat dripped from my forehead. "Well, uh, do you have a minute to talk about our Lord, Jesus Christ?"

"For you, I think I do," she said, reaching for my tie. "Why don't you come inside where it's nice and cool?"

"Come inside?" I asked, voice cracking. "Um, sure."

"Good boy," she said, pulling me in, the door closing behind us.

Wendy led me to the dining room and shoved me into a chair. Grabbing one for herself, she slid it extra close, our knees practically touching. I rested my hand on the Bible as we spoke, pamphlets open on the table.

"So," she said. "What's it like being a Mormon boy?"

"Well," I said, clearing my throat. "As a newly appointed elder it's my duty to teach, expound, and exhort in the name of the church."

"A real multitasker, huh? That'll come in handy when you're married and have to fuck all your wives."

I stared in silence. There was a tingling in the pit of my stomach. My loins warmed from a sudden rush of blood. I prayed for the feeling to pass.

"I'll be honest," she continued. "Most men can barely satisfy one woman. Take my daddy, for instance. Old fart needs a pill just to get it up for five minutes of missionary. But you, being so young and pent up, I bet you can fuck for hours."

My prayers went unanswered. I could feel myself rising within my pants. Wendy noticed, biting her lip as I squirmed in my seat. "I ought to be getting back now," I said.

"But you just got here," she said, leaning in, hand on my thigh. "Didn't you want to open my mind to the Lord?" The robe fell slack around her left shoulder. Her knees slowly widened. "Maybe make me spread my legs for Him?"

I shot to my feet. "No, we can't," I said, backing against the wall. Wendy approached like a lioness stalking prey. I hugged the Bible to my chest. "Premarital sex is a sin."

"I know that, silly," she said, her fingers dancing up my shirt. "I would never want my pussy to get you in trouble." Her warm breath perked my ears as she whispered, "That's why you're going to fuck my ass instead."

"I, uh, I..."

"Shh, it's okay," she said, putting a finger to my lips. Prying the Bible from my hand, she dropped it beside herself, then balled my tie in her fist. "Come with me."

Submitting to temptation, I followed her, each step distancing me further from my faith. We entered her bedroom. Sin prevailed. God was dead.

"Cut!" the director yelled from offscreen. With the utterance of that single word, the illusion was shattered. This hadn't been a test of will or a cruel loss of faith, after all. "Good stuff," he continued. "Prep for sex while we light the bedroom. No stills today, we'll go straight to hardcore and bang this thing out. Back up in ten."

Wendy Waves and I broke character and walked back to the dining room. The director, Don Keedic and his production assistant, Benji, flicked off the light kits and unplugged the cables, casually moving the stands and tripods into the bedroom while debating the best angle from which to shoot the sex.

Don Keedic was a thirty-something freelance director and, like me, was a film school dropout. Efficient and versatile, he ran sets for numerous studios every week. Benji was Don's right hand. More than just an assistant, he was also a boom operator, which meant he listened to every wet squelch with graphic clarity and then had the honour of cleaning up after it all. A P.A. was often a thankless job, but Benji remained cheerful, maybe because of the naked women around him every day or the fact that he was perpetually stoned. His family owned a weed farm up in NorCal and Benji was known around town as a reliable plug, his social media littered with half-naked porn stars holding jars of flower and rolling blunts on top of exposed asses and tits.

"Could I have the bucket, please?" Wendy asked no one in particular.

"Sure can, dollface," Benji's voice called out from the bedroom. He appeared with a shower caddy filled with various lubes, baby wipes, condoms, paper towels, douches, and other tools of the trade. "Still down for that interview later, right?" he asked Wendy.

"Duh, of course," she said.

"My followers are gonna love you!" He left the bucket with us and returned to the bedroom.

Wendy reached in and pulled out a pre-packaged disposable enema. "Gonna do my girly stuff and clean out again just to be safe, although I should be totally clean. I haven't eaten, like, *anything* since last night. I'm a total perfectionist, you know, especially now that I'm, like, known as an anal superstar."

It was true; with box covers, centerfolds, and award nominations, Wendy was quickly becoming an it girl of porn. She trotted off to the bathroom while I sifted through the bucket for a pack of baby wipes. Alone in the dining room, I dropped my pants and gave myself a once over. Then I bit half a Viagra that had been burning a hole in my pocket all morning, letting it dissolve under my tongue before washing down the chalky residue with water. I'd learned to always have one on me and ready to go when the time came so I wouldn't have to open my toiletry bag and alert everyone to the sound of pills rattling. Not that it was any big secret— every male performer of my generation used enhancements. There's maybe a handful of guys who were born to fuck on camera *au naturel,* but for the rest of us, all I can say is Thank God for pharmaceuticals. Personally, I had no reservations about juicing— I appreciated the boost. The only drawback was an occasional stuffy nose or pounding headache. I'd occasionally made the mistake of taking too many pills: my vision would become blurry, pulse racing, head like a balloon. I'd curl up on the cold floor of my bathroom whimpering while my skull tightened around my brain like a cinch. In time, I learned to dial it back. Half a pill was usually enough, although I always kept the second half in my pocket just in case. Still, I preferred to maintain a sense of illusion: "Porno Magic" as I'd come to call it, even if the "magic" was evident in my bloodshot eyes and rosy cheeks.

Ten minutes later, the scene was lit. Wendy and I got down to business, groping and disrobing in front of the camera. She took out my cock and let it grow in her hand before putting it in her mouth.

"Oh yeah, just like that," I said.

"No," Don called out. "Enjoy it less. This should be conflicting for you. I want to see that struggle."

"Oh, okay, sorry," I said, frozen in the moment, halfway into Wendy's mouth.

"Camera's rolling," said Don. "Action!"

Wendy sucked and I looked away in shame. "I am weak," I said. "I have failed you, Lord."

"Good stuff," said Don. "Another minute then transition."

Wendy held her breath and crammed me down her throat. Her face smothered against my belly. Eyes bulging, she pulled back gasping for air. Thick tendrils of sticky white kept us tethered. God's Glue. Wendy looked up: red lipstick smudged, black mascara streaked across her face; a fallen angel.

"Are you ready to sodomize me?"

"If that's what it takes to rid you of the devil," I said. "Then goddamnit, I will."

Wendy turned around and arched on all fours, spreading her cheeks. I positioned behind her and slid inside, making sure Don had a clear view of every inch of the first penetration. After a few gentle thrusts we built up a rhythm. Faster. Harder. Deeper.

"Give me a pull-out," said Don. "Show me the gape."

Balls deep, I did as I was told, slowly exiting Wendy's ass. Only, I wasn't alone.

"Oh shit," I said.

"Cut!" yelled Don. "We got a mess."

I remained calm, eyes to the sky. This wasn't the first time I was shit on. I'm a male performer; it's an occupational hazard. Wendy, however, entered panic mode, cursing at herself as she grabbed another enema from the bucket and ran off to the bathroom. Benji sheepishly handed me a roll of paper towels, his shirt pulled over his nose.

Minutes later, Wendy returned, glossy eyed, offering apologies and genuine shock at what happened. She sat back on the bed, and I put my hand on her thigh, smiling. Don assured her it wasn't a big deal because it honestly wasn't, but it was time to move on and get back to work. "We have such a strong intro," he said. "Plus the five or so minutes of sex we already got. We can do this, we only need like ten more minutes of good anal and we're set."

Wendy agreed to another position. We nestled together in spoon. My arms wrapped around her, sensual and slow. It worked. Until it didn't. There was another mess.

"What the fuck!" cried Wendy.

"It's okay," I said. "We're only human, these things happen."

"Not to me, I'm supposed to be an anal superstar!"

"Sweetie, it's fine," said Don. "We're all professionals here, nobody's judging you."

The tears fell anyway, and Wendy's body convulsed with a sob. She wanted to be anywhere but here. Soon she caught her breath and motioned for Don to sit beside her. He rubbed her back and did his best to console her with compassion and compliments. Benji put in his earbuds and watched YouTube videos on his phone.

I was at a loss. Naked and without anything to do, I went soft. I felt if I stayed in that awkward space for too long, I'd lose the will to fuck, pill or no pill, so I did the only sensible thing I could think of and slid over to an isolated part of the bed. I laid on my back and closed my eyes, tugging myself to a fantasy of better days so I could regain the edge.

Plain and simple, my job was to get hard and fuck whomever I was told, wherever I was told, for however long I was told, until I was told to cum. With everyone's payday in the balance, a location rented by the hour, and a very hungry and exceedingly sensitive starlet on the verge of a breakdown, the last thing we needed was wood trouble.

Wendy dried her eyes and went to the bathroom to clean out one final time. We started a fresh position—The Pile-Driver. It was neither comfortable nor flattering, but at least with her back against the headboard and her legs swung over her head, Wendy had gravity on her side. I was able to fuck her doing half-squats for two minutes at a time before my knees would start to buckle. After some start and stop, there was enough footage for the pop. Wendy got a mouthful and smiled at the camera. Cut. She spat onto the floor and walked off. The lights were killed, stands disassembled, cases packed. Benji collected the bed sheets and loose baby wipes. There were no selfies, no interviews. Don cut our cheques, and we all got the hell out of there as fast as we could. Another day in paradise.

TWO

I said my goodbyes and flashed Wendy a peace sign while she smoked a cigarette on a patio chair outside, flanked by oversized Hello Kitty luggage, her eyes shielded by sunglasses.

Duffel bag over my shoulder, I made my way to the street. Don had asked me to park my car away from the house because it "looked out of place," which didn't surprise me. It was a clunky mid-aughts Nissan Maxima, a hand-me-down from my parents: the car I drove cross country to start my new life out west. With torn leather seats and a rattling engine, it had seen better days. I walked down the block to find it roasting in the sun. The A/C was on the fritz, so I rolled down the windows to cool off the broiling interior. The usual set of warning lights—tire pressure and wiper fluid—greeted me when I turned the key.

I drove toward the one-eighteen, the first of four freeways I'd take to make it through the valley and over the Hollywood hills to my town of Little Armenia. On a good day the trip took an hour, but right now it was the midday rush and every road was flooded with a sea of brake lights. I'd be lucky to make it back by sundown.

I used to live in the valley along with most of the other porn folk. It had its perks, the proximity to work and easy access to beaches being prime examples, but there wasn't much else in the way of incentive. The valley was too sprawled out, too suburban for my tastes. I couldn't help but feel detached from the rest of the city. If I was going to live here, I wanted the true L.A. experience.

When my lease ended, I'd packed up and moved into a one-bedroom just off the 101 in the heart of Little Armenia: north of Koreatown, west of Silverlake, south of Thai Town, east of Hollywood. Its name was derived from the influx of Armenian immigrants who fled their home country during the genocide of the First World War. Generations of families were born and raised in the houses that still lined the streets. Little Armenia was a dense area. The roads were congested, parking could be a nightmare, and the LAPD routinely conducted helicopter flyovers, but the central location kept me on the pulse of the city. It felt alive.

I reached my exit and circled the block a few times looking for parking. I found a spot in front of a Winnebago on cinder blocks near a group of unhoused people who were collecting and repairing bicycles. They must've had damn near twenty bikes strapped to the camper and scattered along the sidewalk: road bikes, BMXs, and beach cruisers. Some without tires, others without seats or chains. Where they got the bikes or the parts to fix them and what they planned to do with them after was anyone's guess.

I grabbed my duffel bag and locked my car, eyeing a pedestrian underpass that cut through the highway. A man in spattered overalls was inside with rollers and buckets, covering up graffiti and gang signs. Every few days someone was sent out to clean the walls, and without fail, the tunnel would be tagged again by the next morning. The culture couldn't be erased with a fresh coat of paint. Not long ago, a couple mattresses were stacked in front of the tunnel entrance and set on fire. The flames fanned onto the highway and a portion of the road had to be closed until the fire department could hose everything down. I didn't know if the fire was meant as a form of protest or if someone was just fulfilling their pyromaniac desires, but a queen-sized silhouette was now permanently etched into the sidewalk: a charred shadow of the past.

I made it to my building—a two floor, nine-unit complex built in the early '30's. My unit was a front-facing lower with original hardwood floors, 12-foot bevelled ceilings, and a walk-in shower with a separate free-standing tub. I didn't have a dishwasher or a parking space, but who needed amenities when you could rent your own personal slice of history for $1300 a month.

I checked the mailbox. Junk. Inside, then straight to the trash with all of it. A Domino's box sat on my stovetop. I kicked off my shoes and fell onto the couch, gnawing on cold pizza. Above me was a floating shelf with a row of books held in place by my golden AVN statuette. Engraved in its base were the words, *"Best Male Newcomer."* I had won the award for my first year in the business: I was twenty-two, full of hope and promise. I had even booked a room for my parents at the Luxor Hotel in Las Vegas and got them tickets to the ceremony. It was a milestone. I was officially in the porno record books. A winner.

With greasy fingers, I deposited my $500 cheque through my bank's mobile app. Even though I had been shooting full-time for the last three years and was making steady money, my account never seemed to increase past a certain threshold. With an average of twelve shoots a month, I was earning what could be described as a middle-class income, only the middle class was long since dead and buried in America, and nowhere was that fact more evident than in a big city like Los Angeles, where making anything less than six figures was considered below the poverty line. Sometimes it felt like the money went almost as fast as it came, like I was barely keeping my head afloat. I did my best to remain resilient and take it in stride. I was in my mid-twenties trying to make a name for myself in a seriously demanding industry. Life was supposed to be tough.

With this deposit, I now had twelve-hundred bucks in cash. I was a far cry from flush, but I wasn't about to be slumming it with the bicycle boys anytime soon. My bills for the month were paid, the fridge was stocked, I had half a bottle of pills, two days left on my test, and another scene booked for tomorrow. Things were going just fine.

I walked into my bathroom and turned on the shower, giving the water time to heat up as I took off my clothes. While slipping down my boxers, I caught sight of something unexpected—a red blotch of skin at the base of my shaft. I prodded it with my finger. No pain, but it was raised and had a slight itch to it. Chafing from today's scene. I told myself it was nothing to worry about.

Stepping into the shower, the steaming water offered a reprieve, the sins of the day cleansed from my body and sent swirling. Fifteen minutes later, the water was lukewarm. I dried off and inspected my skin again. Bad news. The heat caused the blotch to boil and mutate into a cluster of pus-filled sores, the unmistakable sign of a herpes outbreak. *Fuck.*

Wrapped in a towel and with water beading down my back, I paced the living room, nibbling at my pinky nail as I called my agent, Beverly, to tell her the bad news. Beverly La Bianca was the owner of Paragon Models. She started to represent me midway through my second year, after I fired my first agent, Max Michigan. Max had been good to me. He'd taken a chance on a nobody and practically handed me a career. I wouldn't have won *Best Male Newcomer* without him. But he lost his way. He'd started sending out the wrong call sheets, booking girls for bogus shoots. Blowing rails in the office. Palm Springs every weekend. It got to the point where I couldn't even get him on the phone. One by one his roster quit. It was only business. When I left him, Beverly was ready to welcome me into the Paragon family, arms wide open, pen and contract in hand. Originally from the Bronx, Beverly cut her teeth managing night clubs in the nineties before cashing out and moving to L.A. to open her own agency. With nearly two decades of experience, she helped usher in some of the biggest names in porn and had seen her fair share of wasted potential. She was a nurturing mother-figure to every talent she signed, protecting everyone under her wing. But, above all, she was a shrewd businesswoman. She knew every dime owed to her clients and didn't let anything keep her from collecting. I felt protected knowing I had someone like Beverly on my side, but my stomach tightened knowing I was about to disappoint her.

"Hey sweetie," she said, picking up the line. "How we doin'?"

"My friends are back," I said. "The party crashers."

"*Oh,*" she sighed. "Didn't we just have an outbreak a couple months ago?"

"That's the thing about herpes," I said. "It always shows up at the worst times."

"I'll call the producer and let him know we're cancelling. I'm sure he'll be thrilled."

"Tell him it's out of my control."

"You know, I could lecture you about how problematic it is to cancel at the last minute and the importance of maintaining a good reputation, yadda, yadda, yadda."

"I'm only as good as my last scene."

"See? You've heard all this before. All I can say is better now than tomorrow morning."

"Right. I'm sorry about this."

"Don't worry. You're doing the right thing. Let me know when you're camera ready, all right? Take care of yourself, sweetie."

"Thanks, Bev."

I hung up the phone and dug into my medicine cabinet, taking out two different bottles of pills, Valacyclovir and Lysine. 1000mg of each, three times a day for a week...two weeks...however long it took for the little bastards to dry up and crust over, sent back into hiding until the next time they decided to surface.

It's a hard truth, but even with our standardized testing, STDs happen. Chlamydia and Gonorrhea—I caught them both more than a few times. A shot of drugs to the ass, a z-pack, and I was sent on my way. Herpes was different though. Once I got it, it became a part of me. Always lurking. Always plotting. Bad day at work? Outbreak. Parking ticket? Outbreak. Scratching too hard? Outbreak. New scented body wash? Motherfucking herpes outbreak.

I never did find out who gave it to me, not that it mattered. It's fair to assume every performer has caught or will catch it at some point. Not a question of *if,* but *when.* It's a rite of passage, or so I was told. I knew herpes wasn't a death sentence, but it was a test, something I'd have to learn to live with. Another occupational hazard that came with turning a fantasy into a day job.

For the time being I was resigned to life on the injured list, doing my best to refrain from all things sex lest I risk further breaking the skin and restarting the healing process. I could go long stretches without fucking, but what I struggled with the most was not being able to jack off.

Jacking off was one of my most cherished pastimes. I could waste entire days tucked away in my bedroom at my desk, my screens buzzing, CPUs working overtime. It was a sacred act of self-care through flagellation, an agonizingly long exercise. I loved every minute of it. Time would melt, my gaze glued to the screen, gooning to an abyss of smut in search of the perfect moment, unwilling to waste my seed on just anything. My dick attached to my hand like a needle in a junkie. Upon release, the drug would course like ice through my veins, electricity down my spine, legs lightning rods in a storm, kicking and spasming, my unbuckled belt clanging against itself at my feet. My eyelids would flicker, head jolt back, and I'd released one final gasp before everything went black and I'd fall limp. Outstretched and covered in myself, my shallow breathing would be the only semblance of life before I'd slowly revive as the human parts crept back. I'd grab a worn pair of boxers from my hamper and wipe off. Pulling up my pants, I'd stand and open the window blinds, letting light flood the room. The warmth would envelope me as I absorbed the outside sounds: a neighbour's T.V., cars honking at a double-parked delivery van, police sirens in the distance, spouses arguing next door, children playing in the driveway, dogs barking at the mailman. Hello again, world.

THREE

It would be a while before I could experience the high. I did my best to stay preoccupied—through video games and journaling, mostly. I liked writing, it was one of the few other pursuits I had a natural proclivity for, but it was tough to maintain discipline when every time I sat at the desk my dick was out almost immediately. At the very least, this downtime allowed me a chance to crack open the notebook and fill a few pages. Even still, I couldn't help but undo my pants every few minutes and check the status of my skin, as if the sores would magically vanish. No such luck. The only thing that would make them go away was time. All I could do was take my meds and practice a little patience and positive thinking while the days went by.

Elsewhere, life did continue to have its bright spots. A few months back, my college buddies, Bernie and Lou, had made good on their promises to join me out west. Bernie was an aspiring actor. With his dark Italian complexion, boyish good looks, and a curious mind, he was primed for the big screen. Following a familiar path, he went out on auditions during the day while waiting tables at night in Beverly Hills. Lou was an editor in a post-production house cutting commercials and music videos. His most recent job had netted him fifteen hundred—not bad for twelve hours of work. I could make that amount too, but it'd be from three separate employers, split over three days of production, and with three different sexual partners. Same Same.

They rented an apartment within a new complex in Hollywood, fully equipped with modern comforts like central air and a fitness center, their furniture a mix of Ikea and second-hand thrifts, their walls decorated with movie posters—*Blue Velvet, Hook, Rocky*. Bernie had handwritten affirmations taped around his room and magazine cutouts of all his idols collaged on the inside of his door like a teenager's vision board. Lou's bedroom housed a custom-built PC with dual 27-inch wall mounted monitors, every cord and cable neatly tucked away. His space was minimalist and uncluttered, everything in its right place.

Individually, their styles couldn't be further apart, but with their combined powers they were a dynamic duo. I'd hoped their hometown familiarity mixed with their post-grad hunger would offer me a second wind, a newfound motivation, or at the very least, a welcome distraction. We'd often meet to see movies at the Arclight, or six-dollar matinees at the Los Feliz 3. We'd lounge on the shores of Venice and Manhattan Beach. Sometimes we'd post up at Bernie's restaurant, people watching while sipping comped drinks and picking at appetizers. But, without question, our favourite shared activity was hiking.

For many Angelenos, hiking is much more than just a social outing. It's part of our daily routines, our weekly commitment. Alongside yoga and astrology, hiking is considered a religion around here. It's for those of us who prefer our revelations to arrive through catharsis, our self-growth evident by our sweat stains and the miles logged on our fitness apps. It's how we get pure. It also doesn't hurt that we can get a killer tan at the same time.

The three of us held one of our weekly prayer sessions at Malibu Creek State Park, sufficiently stoned after hotboxing the Maxima.

Today's hike started like any other in L.A.: defined dirt paths, soaring views, distant canyons. All of that was just a prelude, something to get the blood pumping. The real trailhead was two miles in, at the top of a dam marked by a chain-link fence with signs warning *Danger* and *No Access*. It seemed like a dead end, but there was a human shaped hole cut into the fence, taunting, as if to say, *Go ahead, we dare you*. On the other side was the only available option to get down into the brush: a caged ladder.

We made it to the top of the dam and went through the fence. Waking to the ladder, Bernie's water bottle slipped out of his hand. It rolled over the edge and down the ladder, bouncing like a pinball against the rusted metal. A strong gust of wind whipped Lou's hat right off his head and sent it sailing down to the bottom.

"You guys good?" I said. "Let's try and make it down this thing in one piece."

"Agreed," they said.

We descended the ladder, the cliffside growing around us until only a sliver of blue sky remained. The guys collected their lost items, and we set off into the bush. A murky creek guided us across porous moon-like boulders. We hopped from rock to rock, scaling and scrambling. Wooden boards were wedged between exceedingly distant stones, offering thin, splintered passageways across the water. The boards had been placed by good Samaritans—they were human elements added over the years to make the trail more accessible. Previous failed attempts at bridges jutted from below, jagged and moss covered. Out here, humans were at the mercy of Mother Nature.

We found a secluded spot to rest and pass a joint; the air and vegetation were so dry that a single rogue spark would light the entire place up, hundreds of acres burning away within minutes. Who held the power now?

"All right, I got a question for ya," I said, lighting up and taking a rip. "If you had to write and direct your own porn, what would it be?"

I passed the joint to Bernie. "Wowww," he said, taking a pull and holding his breath, contemplating. Exhaling the smoke, he said, "I got the perfect idea, dude, check this out. Post-apocalyptic world, super gritty, right? The water supply is totally fucked, and people are eating, like, bugs and grass. Two survivors realize they have to repopulate the Earth, so they just let out all their anger and fear and sadness of having seen all their loved ones die horribly and shit, like, really just go at it, you know?"

"Fucking for the sake of humanity," I said. "I'd watch it. Don't know if I could jack off to it, but I'd definitely watch."

"Ugh," said Lou, reaching across to grab the joint from Bernie. "The sequels would be super gross and incestuous—the next generation."

"Incest sells," I said. "Well, *fauxcest,* anyway. Been my bread and butter for years."

"I got a great one," said Lou, smoke billowing. "How about, 'There Will be Cum,' starring Daniel Gay Lewis."

"Oh my god," I said. "I can see the cover. A giant cum geyser."

Bernie jumped into character, impersonating an old and drunken Daniel Plainview. "If I have a dick and you have a dick, and my mouth stretches across the room, I suck your dick, I suck it up!"

"I've abandoned my condom," said Lou. "I've abandoned my condom!"

Laughing to ourselves, we heard a rustling from behind.

Lou leapt to his feet. "What was that?"

We turned, and out walked half a dozen lost and confused kids, boys and girls, probably middle schoolers. Their eyes wide, clothes dirty, phones in hand desperately seeking cell service.

"Do you guys know how to get out of here?" one of them asked.

"We saw this trail on Instagram and are, like, totally lost," added another.

"Yeah, it can be a little confusing for a first timer," said Lou.

"But you're on the right path," added Bernie.

"Wanna follow us out?" I asked.

"Yes, please!" said the kids in unison.

I stubbed out the joint. They tagged behind. We led them over more boulders and through some questionably defined paths, all the way to the final hurdle, the gorge, where we faced two options: take the plunge from one of the ten-foot rocks and swim to shore, or defy gravity and climb around the perimeter. The obvious choice would be to jump in and celebrate the end with a splash, but, due to a dry winter, the water had become more than a little stagnant, its surface coated with an unnerving layer of green foam and algae.

The kids were a little behind and we chose to go on without them, figuring they'd catch up with time to watch us and get an idea for themselves. Cautiously, the three of us mounted the rock wall and slowly made our way across, knees trembling, doing our best to stay calm and narrate vague foot holds and grab points as we went. A group of onlookers waiting to climb across in the opposite direction was surely impressed by our bravery. Back on land we met the group, a trio of models, tall and slender, dressed in designer athleisure wear with full faces of makeup.

"Hi, ladies," I said.

"Excuse us," a deep voice called. Appearing from behind one of the models was a man sporting long brown hair in a ponytail, reflective aviators, a scruffy beard, leather strap bracelets, and a flannel shirt with rolled sleeves exposing two matching black triangle tattoos on his forearms. Hipster Jesus.

I smiled and walked past. Lou followed while Bernie moseyed behind by the rock wall. We overheard hipster Jesus complaining to his group about having to wait. Then, in a sudden outburst, he said, "Goddamnit, Stacy. I told you to keep your boots out of the mud. They need to be bone dry or you'll slip. And if I see you on your phone again, I'm throwing it in the water."

I heard a high pitched *"sorry"* in reply.

"Someone's off his meds," Lou joked as we walked toward the banks of the gorge. We sat on the trunk of a fallen tree, a prime position to overlook the action.

Across the water, we watched as hipster Jesus decided there

was no virtue in patience. With swelling arrogance, he forged ahead while the kids still struggled to get their footing on the other side.

"Yo, dude," Lou called out. "I'd wait if I were you."

"Yeah," I chimed in. "There's another group coming and they're not too experi—"

"Hey, peanut gallery," he shot back. "I've been coming here for twenty years. I got it. But thanks for the referee."

Lou and I didn't respond. Instead, we watched him expertly glide across the rocks with such speed and grace it almost looked as if he was floating above them. Like he really had been coming here for twenty years.

"*Jesus,*" said Lou.

I saw Bernie from far, hands on his head, mouth agape in a wide smile. He jogged over to us, out of breath. "Holy shit, I can't believe that just happened. Do you know who that is?"

"A douchebag?" said Lou.

"Bro, that's Jared *fuckin'* Leto," said Bernie.

"Bullshit," I said.

"No bullshit," said Bernie. "Look at him. The long hair, the attitude, surrounded by models. Those arm tattoos are a dead giveaway."

Just then, the middle schoolers also made the connection. The girls squealed in excitement. One of the guys rubbernecked so hard he slipped off the rocks and into the slimy water.

"I'll be damned," said Lou. "Always knew he'd be a prick."

"I have a real gift for this, no?" said Bernie.

"Yeah, you oughta be a tour guide," said Lou. "Celebrity spotting in the wild."

"Who do you think is at the restaurant today?" I asked.

"Only one way to find out," said Bernie. "Let's go, I'm starving."

As we walked off, I took one last look and saw Jared helping the kids get across, taking his time with them and explaining exactly where to put their hands and feet, showing them there was nothing to be afraid of. He was teaching them instead of just leaving them in the lurch like we did.

In the end, maybe the joke was on us.

FOUR

A week later I woke up and found the sores were gone. It was like Christmas morning. I called Beverly to tell her the good news. I was back in the game.

My skin was clean, but my 14-day test had expired. STD testing is one of the very few prerequisites for fucking on camera. That, and two forms of government identification. Up until the mid-2000s, performers only needed to test every thirty days and submit a paper printout of their results. Now we're required to test every fourteen days, effectively cutting the window of transmission in half. Once our results are in, they're automatically uploaded to an online database, our profiles colour coded green or red to indicate our status. Our testing practices are sacred, and while they're far from perfect, they do a good enough job of keeping up safe in the inherently risky business of fucking for money.

I drove to Talent HQ in Northridge. It was a cozy office. A mother and daughter team ran the daily operations, a corner reserved for selfies with festive backgrounds and props updated with the holidays. Talent HQ was open to the public for blood testing, but it catered to performers: the test we bought was even called "The Performer Panel." Blood and urine samples tested for all the majors: chlamydia, gonorrhea, syphilis, and HIV. Next day results. Panels cost $165 each, and they didn't accept insurance. I paid the money, pissed in a cup, and watched my blood snake through tubes and collect in vials. On my way out the door I took a selfie while wearing cupid wings and holding a heart shaped pillow—leftover props from Valentine's Day.

Back home, I wanted to celebrate with a pop, and maybe make a few extra bucks at the same time. I split my computer screen: one side with multiple *cumpilations* queued and buffering, the other half dedicated to Skype. I was ready to log in and see if any of my fans were in the mood for a webcam show.

The relationship between me and any buyer was standard. They'd send a message with what they wanted, and I'd quote them a price. Rates started at $100 to watch me for ten minutes. Special requests required pay bumps. Some fantasies were specific, like jacking off while I peered through my windows and pretended to spy on my neighbour's wife, or dressing as a gym teacher and blowing on a whistle while I came. If they haggled or tried to engage me for free, I'd ignore them. A few minutes of radio silence and they'd relent. Once the money was deposited, I'd turn on my webcam and full screen the muted porn for stimulus as I showed off and talked dirty.

Sometimes a few buyers wanted shows at once. I'd add them to a queue and entertain them one at a time. To maximize profit, I'd avoid cumming altogether in favour of pretending to cum while spraying a few forceful spurts of clean piss at the camera, aiming toward an off-screen towel placed below my feet. I could pull this trick for two or three shows before having the urge to cum for real. If I played it up and moaned right, nobody was ever the wiser, or if they were, they never complained because in their minds they still got their money's worth. People genuinely wanted to believe the fantasy.

When I didn't have paying viewers of my own, I would be the one paying, usually to fellow performers or fetish models—women I had met over the years and kept in touch with. If I was horny and saw they were online, I'd hit them up to talk sleazy as I played on cam. Sometimes they'd offer me an industry discount, but I was no slouch. I always paid for their time. Nobody worked for free. It was my own personal way of churning the porno money mill.

There I was, naked in my bathroom, sitting on the lip of the tub, semi-erect, with a bladder ready to burst, my laptop perched on the toilet seat in front of me, rapid fire cum shots on the screen. I logged into Skype and saw one of my favourite co-workers was available: Venus Reigns, dominatrix. Raven haired and statuesque, Venus made a fortune doing in-person privates. Her specialties included Findom, sensory deprivation, and cock & ball torture. We hadn't met in person, but we were mutuals on Twitter. Venus and I had a playful rapport. She charged a nominal fee, and in return I helped brainstorm degrading phrases and pet names to give her loyal cucks—*Reigntards* being a personal favourite of hers.

At that moment I didn't care about making money. I wanted to cum, and I wanted Venus to be the one to make me do it. Before I could message her though, I was stopped by a fan—a regular of mine—with the username GlazeFace77. They were looking for some stimulation of their own.

"Hi. Show now?" they asked.

"No show," I said. "Busy now."

"No show?"

"Later!"

I closed out of Glaze's chat. Without even messaging, I deposited $30 into Venus' account and called her, my camera aimed at my fevered fapping, knowing full well she wouldn't give two shits about seeing my face. I waited for her to jump into character, spewing her usual stream of filth and grime.

She answered the call sniffling, holding a rag over her left eye. "I'm going to have to let you go," she said. "For good."

"Awe, come on, why?" I asked, oblivious and eager to play.

"I'm going to jail," she said.

"Yeah, whatever," I said, laughing. "Come on, do you want me to cum or what?"

"Logan," she said. "There's blood all over my floor." Venus craned her neck, staring at something off-screen. She let the rag fall. Her eye socket was puffy. She stood and bumped the camera, tilting it toward the floor. I saw what looked like a pair of boots, toes up and splayed as though adorning someone's feet. Venus corrected the camera, her ghost-white face filling the frame, eyes bloodshot. "I have to go." The feed cut out and her username disappeared from my contact list.

Dumbstruck, I tried to process what just happened. She had to have been fucking with me, I thought. Some sort of morbid joke to freak me out before calling back. "You gullible motherfucker," she'd say. "It was just an act!" I mean, you don't kill someone and then answer a Skype call from a pervert ready to piss all over his bathroom; that can't possibly be the first move after murder. The minutes dragged. No call back. Maybe it wasn't too far-fetched of an idea, Venus killing somebody. I knew she had violent run-ins before. I remembered she once cammed with a black eye and a busted lip after getting "Jumped by some psycho," she said. I wondered if it was the same guy. Maybe it was payback, a well thought out plan of revenge. Or maybe it was a crime of passion, self-defense? An overzealous client took things too far, Venus had no choice but to fight back. Then, in a stupor, she would go about her day. Stranger things have happened.

If she were telling the truth, chances are I might be hearing from the police sometime soon. The two of us had communicated, maybe even corroborated in their minds—me with my dick in hand, her with a corpse at her feet. That kind of thing required explanation.

For now, Venus was gone, but GlazeFace77 was still online. The urge to piss was suddenly overwhelming. I reasoned it would be a shame to let it go to waste.

I messaged them. "Still want a show?"

"Yes! Show please!"

"Sure, you know what to do."

I resumed the cumpilations. GlazeFace77 deposited $100 into my account. I turned on my webcam and started the show.

FIVE

I received my clean test results the next morning. Venus was still MIA, her Twitter showing no sign of activity beyond auto-generated tweets promoting sales on websites like ManyVids and Clips4Sale. I decided to put thoughts of her and the body on the back burner. As curious as I might've been, I wasn't living inside of a murder mystery. I was no detective. Some things were best kept locked away and forgotten about. I had enough problems of my own. Plus, rent was due. I had to get to work.

My first scene back was for Derelict Video under the direction of Vic Malice. Vic had entered the business in the early 2000s during the glory days of gonzo. Gonzo was porn with no plot, no script, and no bullshit. It separated itself from other styles in that it allowed the camera to be a participant in the scene, often getting as close to the action as possible. Most scenes started with the female performer stripping. Sometimes she'd introduce herself, but other times her name would appear as a simple graphic on the screen, fading away almost immediately so as not to obstruct the view. She'd play with herself. An anonymous cock would approach. Sex ensued.

I preferred the no frills approach of gonzo. It was raw, un-polished, and had a certain spontaneity to it. It's the type of porn I liked to watch and the type of porn I preferred to shoot. Porn used to be simple. Nowadays, the industry was more concerned with leeching ideas from the mainstream, loosely reconstructing popu-lar movie scenes, and capitalizing on the week's viral videos.

When it wasn't chasing trends, it was pumping out copious amounts of fauxcest. I'd lost count of how many stepsons or stepbrothers I'd played, the stepsisters and stepmothers I'd fucked. People couldn't have sex on camera anymore just because they were hot and willing, it had to be justified with a story. As a result, gonzo had fallen out of fashion.

Vic tried his best to adjust his style to match the changing of the times, but he never gelled with the glamcore scene or the feature circuit. After working for numerous studios that were eventually bought out or went bankrupt, he landed a job directing for Derelict—an unremarkable position. That isn't to say the content they produced was subpar, it just means they operated with shoestring budgets, and they weren't going to be winning awards anytime soon. But that didn't matter. Everyone shot with Derelict, from first timers to performers of the year. Big names would be on set day in and day out, and the reasons they kept coming back were simple: the work was easy, the hours were short, and the cheques never bounced.

That day, the shoot was in a 4-bedroom rancher in a remote part of Chatsworth—the armpit of the valley primarily occupied by warehouses and run-down strip malls. This house was a popular choice due to its cheap rental price of a hundred dollars an hour with no minimum. While the price tag was appealing, it did come at the cost of cleanliness and any sense of elegance or glamour. From the street, the house appeared like any other single-family home, but it was just a shell. Nobody lived there. As far as I knew, the owner—a shambling geezer by the name of Frank, or "Dirty Frank" as we called him—only ever showed up to collect his money and stare at the girls.

Dirty Frank's was a dump. Inside were dusty fake plants, crunchy rugs, a sagging white pleather sectional, and squeaky beds with cheetah-print sheets. A giant velvet high heel shoe chair occupied what would've otherwise been considered the dining room. The cheap laminate floors were so dirty my soles would be black within seconds of being barefoot. Girls would baby wipe their feet two or three times during a shoot—an act for which Dirty Frank was only all too eager to volunteer his services. Unbelievably, some of them even accepted his offer. Maybe that's why he never bothered to clean the floors. The kitchen was used as production headquarters, all the drawers and cabinets empty. Camera gear, laptops, stands, and cases littered the space. Makeup had a corner reserved with a folding chair and a ringlight, brushes, palettes, and sprays strewn across the countertop. Duffel bags and suitcases filled with lingerie sets and high heels lay open on the ground, their innards displayed for Vic to ponder.

My scene was set on the velvet shoe chair. All things considered, it was probably the classiest option. I was paired with a platinum haired goddess by the name of Savannah Lynx. Cosmetically enhanced from top to bottom, Savannah stood head and shoulders above me. I had to crane my neck to see her face. Thankfully, by the time I entered the frame she was already on her knees. I might only be five-foot-seven on my best day, but when shot from the waist down, I could be six-feet tall.

Twenty-five minutes later, I came on Savannah's face; she blew a kiss to the camera, and that's a wrap, a welcome return to form. I was in at 10:30 a.m. and out the door by 1:15 p.m., cheque in hand for a grand total of $400—an amount I couldn't say I was particularly proud of. Sure, it was three hours of so-called work with a woman miles out of my league and the pay was only a hundred bucks less than my last scene, but in my mind five hundred for a day's work had a nice ring to it. Four sounded like I was fucking at a discount. Then again, had the extra hundred been worth getting shit on?

Male performers are not the leads. We aren't top billed. Sometimes we're not even credited for our work. We're mostly regarded as little more than glorified human dildos, but that isn't to say our job is unnecessary. A competent male performer controls the scene like a drummer in a band, we set the pace and keep the rhythm. We find the light and position our partners; we open the penetration to the camera. Most importantly, we communicate with the director via whispers, hand gestures, and cues; knowing when to transition, when to hold, when to pick up the pace, when to pop. Our responsibilities are limited but our role is important. Viewers come for the women, but a good male performer is the faceless hero of porn—there's even an award celebrating the most underrated cock of the year: *Unsung Swordsman*.

I had no delusions about being a star and was realistic about my place in the food chain. I considered myself a mid-tier talent. I was in regular rotation with a few producers, attractive enough to land box covers, and my acting wasn't half bad by porn standards. My performances were strong, but I wasn't without a few short-comings—my height being a prime example. Standing positions against countertops and desks sometimes proved impossible without me struggling on my tip toes or, in some extreme cases, without the assistance of an apple box. One of the most ubiquitous and useful pieces of equipment on a film set, an apple box can be used to prop furniture, level dolly tracks, and make actors appear taller than they really are. It's an old Hollywood trick. Standing on an apple box for dialogue was one thing but needing it so my cock could reach my partner was more than a little emasculating.

Performers aren't unionized, our pay fluctuates based on budget. Sure, I had a rate that I encouraged Beverly to push for, but that didn't guarantee I'd get it. If the answer was no, I could stand my ground and make it clear that Logan Pierce refused to fuck for a penny less, all but closing the door on lower paying gigs. Or, I could swallow my pride, deem the offer to be uncool but fair, and take the job.

Was I undervaluing myself by accepting four hundred and letting producers know my rates were negotiable? The male talent pool was oversaturated as it was. If I wasn't in the scene, it'd be someone else, and maybe they'd do it better and for less. Then where would I be? Begging for scraps with the rest of the mope squad? No, thank you. It might not have been the head chair, but I liked my seat at the table. I intended to keep it. The way I saw it: I was broke and it was money, so who was I to complain? At least I'd be able to pay my rent.

SIX

Being crowned *Best Male Newcomer* wasn't entirely without its perks. Sure, the award itself was a novelty, but it helped to increase my exposure, both in and out of the industry.

One morning I got an email from a guy named Sal Shooter, director of digital content for Pinnacle News, an NYC-based men's lifestyle website that offered tips for buying cigars, stocking whiskey, cooking the perfect medium rare steak, and secrets to seducing women. Most of it was bullshit, but at the time, Pinnacle News was averaging over a million unique visits a month. Sal said they were interested in shooting a "day in the life" segment with a male performer to shed light on a marginalized and often misunderstood line of work. That, and they wanted to appeal to the lowest common denominator by piquing the world's morbid curiosity about porn. I wasn't exactly in a position to be picky about mainstream publicity, so I accepted the offer.

Three weeks later, spring had officially arrived. I was sitting alone at a table for four at the longstanding Los Feliz diner, *Fred 62*, waiting for Sal and his team to join me and begin production on "Male Porn Star: The Logan Pierce Story." It was initially supposed to be a one-day shoot, but the guys wanted an excuse to spend a full week in sunny L.A., so I convinced them to add a couple more days to the schedule. Today, they would follow me on a hike to see what I did in my off time. Tomorrow, we'd shoot a traditional talking head interview at my apartment and then, at Sal's insistence, they'd accompany me on a date with a fellow performer. Finally, on the third day, I was to bring them to set and let them witness how the sausage really got made.

"Logan Pierce, the man of the hour," Sal called out as he strode into the diner with the Pinnacle news video team. Accompanying him were Jameson the cinematographer, and Zac the assistant/boom operator, all of them dressed in various combinations of track jackets, jeans, hoodies, and high-top Jordans. I was in athletic shorts, a hyper-dry t-shirt, and Merrell boots. It appeared we had varying definitions of the term "hike."

"Hope you're ready to break a sweat today, boys. If you want a story, you're gonna have to work for it," I said, only half-joking.

"Bet-bet," said Sal.

After breakfast, we all squeezed into their rental car—a lime green convertible Ford Mustang—and drove to Griffith Park. I could've driven myself, but I didn't want the guys seeing the current state of my car, and I especially didn't want footage of it edited into the documentary. I was going to be revealing enough of myself, I thought. They didn't need to know everything.

I led the team on one of my favourite local paths, the Vermont Trail, a short but intense two-mile round trip with sharp slopes and incredible views. Sal directed Jameson to shoot me while I jogged up and down some of the more aggressive hills, most notably a section with a steep 70-degree incline. I waited as they struggled to carry the equipment up to meet me. Zac fell on his ass and nearly lost a bag of lenses. Sweat soaked and out of breath, they soon came puffing into view, ready to call it a day and head back. I let them know we were still shy of the peak. Less than enthused, they remained steadfast, doing their best to keep up and save themselves from the embarrassment of admitting defeat. Few things motivate a person better than peer pressure. Their skin bright pink and their bodies wavering with each passing step, we reached the summit and were gifted with a panorama of the city.

"Holy...Shit," said Sal between panted breaths. "You can see everything from up here."

With the Hollywood Hills on full display, the downtown skyline in the distance and the shimmering Pacific framing the shot, it was the perfect place for an on-camera introduction. Jameson and Zac cooled off, then set up the camera and microphone.

"Give us a quick intro," said Sal. "Who you are, where you are, and what you do for a living. Something punchy."

I closed my eyes and took a moment to rehearse in my mind.

"Anytime you're ready," said Sal.

I opened my eyes and with smug self-assurance, I looked directly into the camera. "Right now, I'm standing on a cliff overlooking Los Angeles, the factory of dreams. My name is Logan Pierce and I'm a porn star. Welcome to my playground." I held my stare for a beat. My expression softened and I looked toward an off-camera Sal. "How's that?"

"Gold, my dude. You crushed it!"

"One take wonder," I said. "Now, who's ready to get off this rock?"

The next morning, Sal and the guys infiltrated my apartment. Silently judging my taste, the camera lurked, examining my posters and portraits—Francis Bacon prints in the kitchen, a *Boogie Nights* one-sheet above my bed—dirty dishes in the sink, clothes in my wardrobe, capturing all 800 square feet of my home's glory. Jameson shot voyeur footage of me trimming my pubic hair and then showering, cutaways of me detailing each item as I packed my work bag, me looking pensive while I sat in front of an open notebook, me doing pushups next to my couch, and me pretending to jack off while watching porn at my desk.

We sat at my dining room table to conduct a formal interview. "So," said Sal, sitting off camera holding a note of numbered questions. "Who *is* Logan?"

"Out of the gate with a deep one," I said, cracking a smile. "Let's see, Logan is...uh..."

I froze. It shouldn't have been a hard question—Logan is easy going, self-aware. I could have listed a bunch of adjectives like I was reading a job resume, but I knew he wanted me to offer greater insight into the man behind the moniker. I'd never given too much thought to what Logan stood for or what he represented. To me, Logan was nothing more than a name, a thinly veiled extension of myself, a comfortable mask that allowed me to enact my primal desires.

Rather than say any of that I decided to play it cool and repeat an old classic. "Logan is a rebel from the waist down," I said. "Young, dumb, and full of cum."

"Nice!" Said Sal. "That's a perfect sound bite, our viewers are gonna love that."

If I couldn't be insightful, I could at least try to get a laugh, right?

Sal continued. "We saw you at your desk with a notebook. Tell us, what do you typically write about?"

"A little bit of everything, I guess. I mostly journal about daily life, days at the office, good scenes, bad scenes, wild sexcapades. Sometimes I'll experiment and turn them into short stories or scripts."

"Scripts, huh? Ever think about producing them? Working behind the camera?"

"I've thought about it, sure."

"So, you're saying 'Logan Pierce Productions' is in the works?"

"I'm saying if the opportunity presented itself, I'd have some ideas, yeah."

"Bet."

After the interview was over, it was time for the date. A few days before the arrival of Pinnacle News, I put out an APB on Twitter looking for someone willing to be filmed with me at dinner—not the easiest sell, to be honest. I had a history of sour relationships. In my wake lay a trail of one-night stands and failed romances, broken hearts and burnt bridges.

I told Sal it was one thing for a woman to fuck me on camera but being seen out with me on a date was another story altogether. "Yes!" He said, eyes lighting up. "That's the kicker. It'll add some drama to this thing."

Someone did come through just under the wire. A performer named Maya Summers. She was in her early twenties, and of Cuban descent. She had lace bow tattoos on the backs of her thighs and an eye-catching pair of fake tits. A Miami native, Maya was in town on a work trip, staying at her agency's model house in Woodland Hills. She was relatively new, having followed the common path of stripper turned performer—a sure way to earn a solid six-figures. We'd talked briefly on Twitter but hadn't yet met in person. God only knew why she agreed to come. Maybe it was the promise of a million viewers; whatever the reason, I was more than grateful.

The guys and I waited outside the restaurant. Maya arrived wearing fresh white sneakers and a low-cut nude dress under a cropped denim jacket, further emphasizing her enhancements.

"Hello beautiful," I said, going in for a hug. "Nice to finally meet you." I gestured to the guys. "And this is the crew."

"Nice to meet you too. Hi, crew," she said with a wave.

Zac attached lapel mics to our clothes so our conversations could be heard clearly while Jameson shot clandestine footage from across the restaurant, cinema verité style.

As we walked in, Sal handed me his company card. "Dinner is on Pinnacle tonight, you two get whatever you want." He patted me on the back.

"Looks like we're sampling the menu," I said to Maya.

We sat and ordered a round of cocktails—French 75 for her and a mezcal old fashioned for me. I slid my chair over to Maya's side of the table so the camera could see both our faces. We shared a single dinner menu. Our bodies dangerously close, I put my arm around her, and she rested her hand on my lap.

"I really like your dress," I said, my eyes lingering.

"Well," she said, cupping her chest. "I didn't pay ten grand just to hide them away."

The drinks arrived. "I'll toast to that," I said.

"Bottoms up." She clinked my glass and took an extended sip. "So," she said, dabbing her lip dry with her finger. "I have to confess. I was *warned* about you."

"Warned?" I asked, my scalp tingling. "What does that mean? Warned by who?"

"By some of the girls in the model house," she said. "I told them you asked me out on a date, and they said, 'Be careful, don't fall for his charm. He's a dog.'"

Even though I couldn't see his reaction, I was certain Sal was loving this. Here was that drama he wanted.

"Woof," I said under my breath. "Well, you came out anyway."

"I like to make up my own mind," she said.

"I know you've only known me for about an hour now, but what do you think so far?"

"Hm...I like doggies," she said, batting her eyelashes. "Especially good boys."

"I can be a good boy," I said.

"Yeah? Can you be obedient?"

"I can try."

"You'll have to do better than that."

"Put me to the test," I teased.

"Oh, I plan to, don't you worry about that," she said, giving my thigh a healthy squeeze.

After dinner, we met with the guys outside. "That was amazing," said Sal, collecting our microphones. "So good, I don't even want to talk about it yet in fear of ruining the moment. Logan, keep everything you're thinking in your head, and we'll do an interview first thing tomorrow."

They left. I called a car and the two of us went back to my apartment, wasting no time before we headed into the bedroom.

While making out, Maya pushed me away. "Take your shirt off and get on the ground," she said. "On all fours." I complied without saying a word; losing my shirt and falling to my knees, I placed my hands in front of her feet. I looked up, awaiting her next command. She peered down, superior. "There's my little doggy."

She grabbed my discarded shirt and stuffed half of it in my mouth, tugging on it, encouraging me to snarl as I tugged back. "That's it," she said. "Show mommy those teeth." She let go of the shirt and leaned back, pulling the top of her dress down and rubbing her tits. "Does the good boy want a treat?" she asked. I nodded my head, inching forward. She grabbed my face and pulled me in. I worshipped her with my tongue, licking and swirling around each nipple, spit dripping down her chest. I lifted my face to hers and we kissed, exploring each other's mouths, licking each other's faces, and biting each other's necks. She pinned me to the floor. Snaking out of her dress, she climbed on top, sat on my face, and smothered me while I tongued and sucked like it was my last meal.

I pulled down my pants and started to jack off, but she swatted my hands away. "No, no," she said. "None of that. You have a big day tomorrow and you're going to save it for the camera, understand?"

"Yes, master," I said, my face buried between her legs.

"I can't hear you," she said, slapping my stomach.

"Yes, master!"

"Good. Now keep your hands off your cock and eat that fucking pussy."

She continued grinding, using my mouth as a vessel, taking what she wanted. Her legs quivered; my jaw was numb.

My purpose fulfilled, Maya climbed off and laid beside me. Comfortable silence. Resettled nerve-endings.

"You are obedient," she said. "Now be a really good boy and call me a car home."

Once again, I did as I was told, and fought every urge to jack off after she left.

In the morning, the guys arrived in high spirits, ready for another interview.

Cameras rolling, Sal began. "I know it's the big day and I don't want to mess with your process at all, but during the date Maya said she was warned about you. Could you elaborate on that?"

"Let's just say I've had my fair share of failed relationships," I said. "Either I go on a spree of fucking every girl I talk to, or I try to get serious, make a lot of promises, and then break them and fuck it all up. Self-sabotage. Not an uncommon story."

"I guess at least you're self-aware enough to see your faults, a lot of people don't have that ability."

"Yeah, I can see them," I said. "I just can't seem to correct them."

"Do you believe in monogamy?"

I shrugged my shoulders. "I did until I started having sex with strangers for a living. Monogamy is tricky in this business. Everyone has their own definition and boundaries. I guess if I were to put a label on it, I would call myself a believer in emotional monogamy."

"If the right person were to come along, would you consider leaving porn for them?"

"As in, would I quit if my partner asked me to? I can definitely say I wouldn't leave for someone, but if I were with someone and leaving felt like the right thing to do, well, never say never, right?"

"For sure. On a lighter note, the date went pretty damn good, huh? Maya was totally into you. Anything happen between you two after we left?"

"Well, my jaw is a bit sore, I can tell you that much."

Sal smirked, "Bet."

Interview over, we crammed into the lime Mustang and headed to the shoot house. On set, the guys said their hellos and then faded into the walls, Jameson's camera at the ready. There was no more talking. It was showtime.

I played a college student studying for finals. My session was cut short by my stepsister blasting music in the other room. Irritated, I went to tell her to keep it down. Peeking through her bedroom door, I noticed her wearing panties and a tank top, twerking in front of a camera. I became transfixed, my motives changing. I cleared my throat, letting her know I was watching. Embarrassed, she apologized for distracting me, admitting she was filming herself as part of a music video contest. I told her not to worry and offered to take the camera and film it myself. Through a series of increasingly suggestive questions and advances, I convinced my stepsister to get naked, give me head, and let me fuck her doggystyle while she continued twerking on my dick. The scene was a perfectly choreographed dance. I delivered a performance worthy of a thousand hard-ons, the pop-shot a veritable eruption due—in no small part—to last night's edging. Cut. Print.

The guys were ecstatic. "You're an animal, bro," said Sal. "I've never seen anything like that before in my life."

"That was some graphic shit," added Zac.

"Just doing my job," I said with a wink.

After a day on the trails, an intimate look at my home, a candid date, and a hot sex scene, I was sure we had captured an engaging slice of life, but you never know how these things will turn out until you see the final product. All I could do now was wait and hope for the best.

SEVEN

Beverly booked me a scene for the director Phil Holes. Boy/Girl. $500.

I arrived at his Hollywood condo right off Sunset Boulevard. The entryway was lined with framed rock albums and led to an open concept living room with floor to ceiling windows. A modular black sectional and two gothic thrones sat atop Egyptian rugs, a long-mirrored table between them. A disassembled drum kit lay in the corner. In the dining room was a wrought iron chandelier, G-strings dangling from it in remembrance of porn scenes past. The kitchen had a lingering scent of rotten food. Trash cans overflowed with takeout containers, beer cans, baby wipes, and empty douche bottles. Phil's place had all the markings of burnout, but at least the floors were marginally cleaner than those at Dirty Frank's.

In the mid-90s, when he was a twenty-something budding rock musician, Phil started his career as a production assistant. He was paid a hundred bucks a day to, in his own words, "Carry equipment, stare at hot chicks, and wipe down loads." There were certainly less radical ways to make a living while following a dream.

The years went by, and he did his time, working his way up to a camera operator before he began to call the shots and run his own sets. Eventually, his music prospects dried up while porn continued to prosper, consuming his life. Soon he was directing four scenes a day, five days a week. The same houses, the same furniture, the same positions, day after day. Twenty years gone, all the while his drum kit, the once prized possession that took him years to afford and assemble, remained untouched in his condo.

Still, I refused to believe it was only the money that kept him going. I was sure that somewhere deep inside of Phil remained a small spark of artistry and a desire to create something meaningful that he could be proud of.

Today I was paired with a freckled nineteen-year-old by the name of Kinsley Pink. She had a slight southern drawl and a sunny disposition. Kinsley had moved to L.A. from her hometown of God-knows-where, Oklahoma. Book smart, she graduated high school a year early and went on to study osteopathic medicine at OSU. She traded her landlocked state for coastal living, answering an ad that promised ten-grand a month to aspiring models.

Phil sifted through her suitcase and tried to piece together an outfit. I lounged on the couch and admired Kinsley as she took naked selfies in front of the windows. "Can you believe we live so close to the beach," she said. "It's so rejuvenating. And the palm trees! I swear, I'd never seen one before moving here and now they're on every block. They're so beautiful!"

"Hate to break it to you, sweetheart," Phil said, looking up from a tangled knot of tube socks and thigh-highs. "All the palm trees here are imported."

"Oh," she said, face dropping. She returned to her phone, shrugging off his comment and flashing a smile to her camera. "They're still beautiful to me."

Our scene was an old classic: the naughty schoolgirl. I played a strict teacher and Kinsley a mischievous student. She failed to hand in her assignment, I threatened punishment, one thing led to another, and we fucked each other's brains out on top of my "desk," which was really Phil's dining room table.

"Porno logic" he said about it. "Nobody cares." Maybe pride was overrated.

During the scene I noticed the windows in Phil's condo were directly across from a strip of offices that I could peer into and witness life at its most mundane: suits and ties toiling away in cubicles, doing their best to appear busy in front of their bosses until it was time to clock out and shed the corporate uniform, living free for a few precious hours before doing it all over again.

Being that I could see into their work lives, I wondered if they could see into mine, two people fucking on top of a dining room table while a bozo in a faded cutoff *Master of Puppets* t-shirt circled them with a camera. I already knew the answer. The scene had started with all the office windows wide open, but by the time we set up the pop, all the blinds were drawn. Apparently not everyone was a fan of us flaunting our business, but that's Hollywood.

Our final position was reverse cowgirl. The plan was to fuck until I was close, then I'd squirm out from underneath and finish on Kinsley's face. During our first attempt, right as we were about to transition, Phil suddenly yelled, "Hold it! Low Battery." He darted into his office to grab a replacement, cursing, "shit, shit, shit." On take two, a firetruck and ambulance sped past, their sirens blaring from the streets below. "Goddamnit," said Phil, cutting the camera and rubbing his temples. "I need to piss. Back in a flush." He put down his camera and walked off, leaving Kinsley and I alone.

We continued to fuck. I held Kinsley's wrists as her hands dug into my chest, her feet arched on top of my thighs. All of her weight on me, my body used as leverage. She was in control, and I was on the verge. Too close. By the time I realized what was happening all I could do was pull out and squeeze as hard as possible to plug the seal, but it was too late.

Phil walked in just in time to witness the silky ropes cover Kinsley's pelvis and torso, not a single drop caught on camera.

"First day on the job?" He sighed, hands on his hips. He spun his finger in the air, "Work up another one if you can."

Foregoing the transition, Kinsley dropped to her knees and I stroked in front of her open mouth, panting as I concentrated. One minute passed, then another, and another.

"Any day now," said Phil, glancing toward me as sweat dripped down my face and onto my lips. I licked it away and closed my eyes. I could feel his stare burning. I stroked faster, half-mast, mind foggy. Still nothing. The tension grew. I had lost the edge.

"Sorry," I said, letting go, my skin raw. I palmed away sweat. "I can't do it."

Phil cut the camera and covered his face with his hand. Kinsley closed her mouth, wiped dried spit from her lips and looked toward Phil for guidance. He shook his head. "I'll get the Cetaphil."

It might be an undignified exit, but plenty of pop shots are faked, and not just the obvious ones for stills with yogurt thick rails spread neatly along the face or body. The process for faking in video varies, but most of the time it involves the female talent holding a mouthful of semen-like substance—piña colada mix if they're lucky, or, in this case, Cetaphil face wash if they're not.

The scene cut to me already in Kinsley's mouth. Phil's camera focused on my exaggerated O-face before tilting down to reveal the gooey aftermath. Kinsley drooled out the soapy mix and did her best not to gag. With that, the day came to a lackluster close. We cleaned up, got dressed, and went on our way.

"I swear it won't happen again," I promised.

"Yeah, sure thing, kid."

Walking to my car, I got a text from Bernie. "Wanna get pure at Runyon?"

Runyon Canyon is a tourist destination on every L.A. traveller's bucket list. It's a hot spot for celebrities and influencers. The trails hardly present much of a challenge, but it's still a hike. I was already in Hollywood and had my work bag with me which always had at least one athletic outfit in case the scene called for it. It'd be good to release some steam and break a sweat. I found a spot on Bernie's block and got changed in my back seat. He met me and we jogged a half mile to the trailhead off Fuller Ave.

"So how's auditioning going?" I asked.

"Oh, great," said Bernie. "Yeah, yesterday I read for a commercial about frozen meat delivery, right? The line was 'We guarantee you'll enjoy our succulent cuts of beef.' I said, 'We guarantee you'll enjoy our succulent *cunts...*' and then I just stared, totally frozen."

"Oof, that's a Freudian slip if I ever heard one."

"And I know that shit will come back to haunt me if I ever see that casting director again."

"Like in *Entourage*. Johnny Drama and the cell phone."

"Exactly," he said, jumping right into character, *'Beady eyed little jerk-off.'* He cleared his throat. "Anyway, what's up with you? How was your scene?"

"Started off strong, kinda flaked out at the end," I said. "Made a rookie mistake and popped when the camera wasn't on."

"No! You? How does that even happen?"

"We were fucking in between takes and I got careless," I said.

"But you've dealt with that before, right?" He asked. "I bet you bounced right back like it was nothing."

"Ha, *yeah,* you know me."

"Lucky bastard," said Bernie. "What I wouldn't give to be in your shoes for a day. They must treat you like a prince on set."

"You saying you're not treated like royalty at the restaurant?"

"Far from it," he said. "Tips are good, I guess. But I could do without all the rich assholes and their rich asshole entitlement. The other night, I had a guy send back an order of fries twice— once because they were too soft, and then again because they were too crispy. And he's giving me lip like I'm the one back there frying them. I got so fed up that my manager Craig had to step in and handle it. Comped his drinks. It's always the same thing, people act shitty so they can get freebies."

We reached the peak just as the sun was setting. Dozens of other hikers stood around us and took advantage of the light by snapping selfies and Facetiming.

"Craig took me into the kitchen to calm me down," he continued. "When I told him why I was so pissed he looked me in the eye and said, 'It's not worth the energy. Remember, it's only French fries.'"

"That's sage advice," I said. "Don't sweat the small stuff."

"Simple but effective, right?" Bernie's face was cloaked in golden haze. "It's like my new mantra. Even got it tacked up on my wall. If things feel too heavy, I just take a deep breath and remind myself: *at the end of the day, it's only French fries.*"

EIGHT

At one time Los Angeles may have been considered the porn capital of the world, but internally, the city had been waging a war against the industry for years.

There had been countless forms of government propositions and bills pushed to minimize and constrict the amount of content that was allowed to be shot within the city and the methods by which it was produced. Most bills had failed to pass, but every voting season a new one appeared on the ballot and threatened our livelihoods. The message was clear: the porn industry was slowly being forced out of L.A. In turn, Las Vegas had taken up the mantle, becoming host to numerous studios thanks to the more affordable cost of living and the relatively laxed production restraints. With work trips becoming more frequent, it sometimes felt like I was shooting more scenes out of state than within the eponymous porn valley.

I wasn't much of a Vegas guy. I was an unlucky gambler, the summer heat was unbearable, and the overall vibe of the city was too gaudy for me. Most of all, I hated flying back and forth. I suffered from terrible aerophobia, breaking out in panic sweats at the slightest bit of turbulence. No matter how many flights I took, each one always felt like it'd be my last.

I developed a routine to calm my nerves. I always made it a point to keep a water bottle in the netted pocket attached to the seat in front of me. During takeoff I'd put in my headphones, find the loudest music, and crank the volume to eleven, drowning out mechanical noises and crying babies, numbing my mind until I'd see the flight attendants begin their drink service. At this point, I'd loosen my grip on the armrests and turn my music down, switching tracks to something more mellow. Then for the duration of the flight, I'd watch the water bottle. On a smooth trip, the water barely sloshed, especially when compared to an average drive across town. Maybe it was a false sense of security, but the lack of movement lulled me into believing everything would be all right.

I was flying to Vegas to shoot for Darling Entertainment. Darling had treated me well over the years, keeping me busy with a steady stream of gigs. I was booked to shoot with them for two days, working with the same girl twice, a female talent by the name of Naomi Blonde. I hadn't worked with her before, but one look at her Twitter profile confirmed she was a hard-bodied twenty-something with tanned skin and blonde hair.

I got tested two days before the flight, my Talent HQ profile green with approval. The morning of, I checked my bag, boarded the plane, and took my seat, placing my water bottle in the net pocket. I queued up Nine Inch Nails' *Broken*, closing my eyes as the industrial metal blasted in my ears. We took off and I stared intently at the near-motionless water. An hour later, we touched down in Vegas.

As I was walking toward the baggage claim, my phone rang. It was Darling's production assistant, Wyatt, a vaping nut who carried various batteries, tanks, and E-juice flavours in a customized belt holster.

"Logan, my man," he said. "How ya doing? How was the flight?"

"Uneventful," I said. "Just how I like 'em."

"Cool, cool," he said. "Yeah, so anyway, got a question for ya. Naomi says she's been shooting nonstop and was too busy to get retested for today. Her 14-day is expired but her 30-day is still good. That cool with you?"

"How expired is she?" I asked.

"Five days," he said.

"Five days? And she's been shooting all week?"

"That's what she said, yeah."

"Did you guys just find out about this, or did you deliberately wait until after I landed to tell me?"

"I don't know, man. They just told me to call you."

"Right."

"So...what do you think?"

I paused. In the grand scheme, was working with someone five days past a somewhat arbitrary expiration date really that big an issue? Was I any more likely to catch something outside of the fourteen-day window than within it? It's still unprotected sex, and as far as I was concerned, the risk remained the same whether it's one day after testing or nineteen. But since the start of my career, fourteen-day tests had been the standard. Why feign ignorance now for the sake of convenience? The rules were in place for a reason and the only way to enforce them was to set a precedent.

"I'll call you back," I said, hanging up the phone to call Beverly. In times like this it's best to let the agent handle it and work for her commission.

"Hey sweetie," she said. "A phone call on the day of? Something's wrong."

"How'd you guess?"

"I wouldn't be any good at my job if I didn't know the signs. What's up?"

"I just landed," I said. "Wyatt called me and told me the girl hasn't retested and her 14-day is expired. It feels like they're sand-bagging me."

"How many days?"

"At least five."

"That's bullshit," she said. "Everyone needs a 14-day test."

"Exactly, but they're not giving me much of a choice here."

"Can't they just switch her out for another girl?"

"I doubt it. I'm supposed to work with her today and tomorrow."

"Christ. Which agency is she with?"

"Malibu, I think."

"Wow. Does not surprise me," she said. "*Milo* is up to his old tricks."

"I don't know what to tell them," I said. "If I say I don't want to shoot they'll probably charge me for the day and make me pay the girl's kill-fee, right?"

"You're not paying a cent," she said. "The girl can't just show up with an expired test and expect everyone to be okay with it. It's her fault, and it's Milo's fault. If anyone is going to pay, it's that asshole. Let me call them. Sit tight." Beverly hung up. I collected my bag from the carousel and found an empty seat to wait in with my thumb up my ass.

Malibu Models (located in Chatsworth) was a notorious agency. In its heyday, it was home to prolific female performers like Lexi Belle and Alexis Texas. Then it was sold to new owners and passed around before winding up in the hands of a former suitcase pimp named Milo Magnus—a shiny bald-headed English-man with a permanent constipated grimace on his face. He looked like he had never smiled a day in his life. His strategy was to coast on the company's former reputation while aggressively signing new girls to dubious five-year contracts, encouraging them to lease luxury cars and get plastic surgery to maintain the porn star façade. Once he had them indebted, he pushed them into escort-ing. For Milo, porn was just a front, a means of promotion for his backdoor businesses.

A few minutes later Beverly called with news that the shoots were now cancelled and Darling was booking me a flight back home. Two days of work lost, but at least I did the ethical thing and didn't break procedure—that had to be worth something, right? I assumed as much because I didn't hear another word about it.

A month later, I flew back to Vegas to shoot for Darling. This time I was paired with a newcomer named Cherry Sweets. Curiously, she was represented by Malibu Models. Beverly hadn't raised any concerns so I wasn't worried about it. I boarded my flight, expecting everyone to have learned a lesson and for bygones to be bygones.

Upon landing, I got a call from Wyatt. I instantly knew something was wrong. He said Milo had just called, screaming at them through the phone about how Cherry wouldn't be working with me today or any day, and that Logan Pierce was officially on the No-list for Malibu models. Naturally, the slimy weasel had waited until the last minute to say anything at all.

I played by the rules and respected the protocols, but *I'm* the one who got the boot. Sure, Darling could see how wrong it was to screw me over and how much of a prick Milo was to do what he did, but the simple fact was, Milo owned a talent agency. He was the gatekeeper to a plethora of pussy. For Darling, cutting ties with him would mean losing out on all that potential income. I was male talent earning half as much as my co-star. I was a day player, an afterthought—another disembodied penis in front of their cameras. To them, I was expendable. Everything always came down to the almighty dollar.

Beverly was at least able to hassle Darling for a kill fee for both trips, netting me a grand total of $500 for my lost time, minus her ten percent, of course.

NINE

Back in town, I immediately hit the shores of Venice: a subculture all its own. The boardwalk seethed with families, freaks, and freeloaders. Dispensaries offered pre-rolls and one-hitters to new clients. Wannabe rappers accosted tourists to buy their CDs, music unheard. Crust punks fished for change with paper cups attached to sticks. Artists sold sculptures made from discarded glass found along the beach. Street performers passed around donation buckets, revving up the crowd while breakdancing and doing front flips over each other. And then, in the midst of it all, there were those of us who just wanted to roast in the sun and soak in the ocean.

I went into one of the dispensaries and bought a bag of ten 30mg peach rings. I ate two of the candies and spent a couple hours in euphoria, sunbathing and body surfing, temporarily forgetting my troubles back in the real world.

My phone rang. It was Sal Shooter. I assumed he was calling about my documentary, maybe with a few notes or updates.

"Yo brother, what's good?" he said.

"Getting a tan at the beach," I said. "What's up with you?"

"Guess who's back in town."

"No shit? You guys shooting another piece?"

"You know it, brother—a twenty-year-old chick who's a jet pilot. She's *hot*. And guess what, she wants to meet you! What do you think, can you spare a couple hours and be our guest of honour today?"

"I don't know," I said. "*Maybe* I could fit it into my schedule. Where you guys at?"

"Hawthorne Airport. You familiar? It's like twelve minutes from LAX."

"Never heard of it, but if that's the case I should only be like thirty minutes out."

"We're wheels up in an hour."

"All right, give me a few and I'll head over."

"Bet."

I couldn't imagine what exaggerations Sal had told her to build up my character, but the intrigue was enough for me. She wanted to meet *and* she's hot? I was in—aerophobia be damned.

I chugged the rest of my water bottle, packed up my stuff and headed to my car. With the windows down, the rushing wind ruffled my hair and roared in my ears as I gunned across the 405 Freeway.

Suddenly, the lights on the dash flickered and the car decelerated. I pumped the gas pedal, but nothing happened. Thinking quickly, I merged into the right lane, threw on my hazards, and pulled off onto the shoulder. I slowed to a stop, and all the lights went out. I tried turning the key, but there wasn't so much as a sputter from the engine. No idling vibrations: radio silence. The Maxima was officially dead.

Not wanting to sit in my now-lifeless hunk of junk as other cars whizzed by, I jumped out and found a small grassy knoll a few yards away. I sat on a tree stump surrounded by trash and weeds. Floating orbs of insects hovered above. My mouth was dry from the salty waters, skin simmering from the midday sun, my body hollow from a lack of food. I was wearing pink Hurley board shorts, white flip-flops, and, in bold print, my graphic T-shirt bore the word: **RECKLESS**.

I texted Sal, and to save face, I said my car got a flat tire and they should take off without me. "You'll be missed, brother," he replied.

I didn't have a AAA membership, so my next call was to my insurance company to have them send a tow-truck. Fifteen minutes later a truck came, but it wasn't the one they said to expect. This was a different truck; it was owned by the city, and therefore couldn't do jack-shit for me. The driver said some of his coworkers had passed by and saw my car. Thinking it was abandoned because I was nowhere in sight, they told him to come take a look.

"Sounds like you got a busted alternator," he said. "Wish I could help, I really do, but I'm sure your truck will probably come soon." He drove off, abandoning me with no food, no water, no money, and no hope. I knew none of that was his fault, especially the money, but still.

The minutes ticked by. I was growing delirious when another large tow truck appeared, bringing with it a storm of dust as it pulled onto the shoulder. The dust settled; I noticed AAA decals painted across the cabin doors. I sensed something was off, but like most other bad omens in my life, I regarded it as trivial.

The driver strapped up my car and we were off. As we exited the highway, he got a call from his boss, confirming what I already knew to be true: I wasn't a card-carrying AAA member. The result, he concluded, was that he'd either have to charge me $150 for the tow, or I could call Allstate again and figure out why they sent out a members-only service. I picked up the phone and dialled. They offered to call another truck. Meanwhile the current driver had no choice but to leave, dumping me and the car in a strip mall in Inglewood.

I was stewing inside my metal coffin when a shirtless man in flip-flops, plaid shorts, and a fedora barreled past, toward one of the storefronts. He reached the door of a Little Caesar's before he doubled over and released a torrent of puke, red chunks spraying everywhere. I didn't know if it was blood or fruit punch, but after his insides were on the outside, he spat a final loogie, then sauntered away, leaving some lowly employee with the undignified task of cleaning it up. I watched this poor kid trudge in and out of the store half a dozen times carrying plastic quart containers filled with soapy water, splashing it against the ground toward the street in a desperate attempt to make it disappear. It seemed there were hard times everywhere.

As a crimson river flowed nearby, the correct truck finally came and the driver loaded my car onto the flatbed. I climbed into the cabin and considered my options: I could have him take me back to Little Armenia, drop my car in front of my apartment, get stoned and deal with everything later, or I could have him bring me to the nearest shop and bite the bullet then and there. Decisions, decisions.

I did what I thought was the most logical thing and called the nearest Pep Boys. The voice on the other end told me a new alternator would run around $250 for parts and labour. Not so bad. We went straight to the garage, and with measured care, the driver released my car into one of the assigned waiting spots.

"Hey man, hope it works out," he said, honking his horn as he drove off.

I went inside and talked to a mechanic. He added my name to the list.

"How far down am I?"

"Well," he said, scanning the names. "If you want to wait around, we could probably get to it tonight, but it would be toward the back end, like closing time."

"What time do you close?"

"Nine, nine-thirty depending on how much work we got."

I checked my phone. It was 5:30 p.m. Peak rush hour. I was all the way across town. It'd take me at least an hour and a half to get home, and then I'd have to get another car an hour later. $50 each way. Fuck that.

"I'll wait," I said, peering out the lobby window toward a nearby McDonald's.

I left my keys and meandered to the golden arches where I

wasted time scribbling in my notebook and thumbing through my phone. I picked at a Big Mac and fries while nursing a spicy Sprite. Eventually, the clock approached 9 p.m. I bought two McDoubles to go.

Back at the shop, the mechanic had bad news. They didn't get to my car in time, I'd have to come back the next afternoon. He also hit me with a new quote. Now the estimate for parts and labour was $600. So much for the kill fees. More money that was never really mine in the first place.

I went home, locked my doors, and drew the blinds. I scorched a fresh bowl and hosted a pity party for myself, eating my leftover fast food naked at my desk after I jacked off.

The following day, after I picked up the car, I talked to Sal. Apparently, heavy winds had forced the pilot to land prematurely. They attempted a second run but only lasted a few minutes in the air before descent was "Absolutely fucking necessary. It was *wild,* man, you should've been there."

"Yeah, so sorry I missed it," I said, imagining just for a second what might've happened if I had been there. Maybe my weight would have made all the difference. Maybe the plane would have plummeted in a fiery explosion. I wondered if my car breaking down was what allowed us all to narrowly escape death in a flying tin can. Then I stopped, because these weren't the types of things a person should think about. But if it was true, it would be one hell of a silver lining.

TEN

I got a text from Beverly. "Hey, Don Keedic wants to book you for a shoot this Friday, but first wants to make sure you're cool with the female talent."

"Who is it?"

"Wendy Waves."

"...It's not another anal scene, is it?"

"Nah," she said. "It's a simple boy/girl set-up with a page of dialogue. Your call.

I thought about it for a minute. I had no ill will toward Wendy. Performers were vulnerable, exposed and often asked to do the impossible, like defy human physiology. When small things go wrong, it's only natural to overreact. Some might've wanted us to believe we're only as good as our last scene, but I chose to approach each day as a clean slate and with a clear mind. The past is dead. Besides, everyone deserves a second chance.

"Let's do it," I said.

I showed up to set around eleven in the morning. Don and Benji were setting up lights in the living room. I filled out my paperwork on the kitchen island and brought my bag into the master bedroom which was serving as the makeup suite. Wendy was having foundation applied and making jokes with Gia, the makeup artist.

I recognized Gia right away, but I wondered if Wendy was aware she was in the presence of porno royalty. Gia had been a performer back in the early 2000's—a gonzo girl, as hardcore as they come. She was famous for being the first on-screen recipient of the legendary donkey-punch. I heard a rumour that she once overdosed the night before an AVN ceremony and still made it to the show on time to collect her award, shouting into the microphone, "How's that for a comeback, bitch!?" She had since retired from the partying, starting a family while working part-time as a freelance hair and makeup artist.

"I'd really love to start doing more prosthetic work," she said to Wendy while spritzing her face with setting spray. "You know, like FX makeup for horror movies, exposed viscera and all that." Hardcore indeed.

Within the hour the set was lit. Wendy got into wardrobe, rainbow tube socks and white panties beneath an unbuttoned dress shirt. The scene was titled, "My Best Friend's Daughter." The plot was a carbon copy of our first, only instead of playing a Mormon boy, I played a businessman who also happened to be Wendy's dad's best friend. I was in the neighbourhood working on a new project and stopped by for an impromptu visit. My best friend wasn't home, but his daughter was. She invited me in, and within minutes we did the only plausible thing people can do in that situation: we fucked like animals.

Wendy crawled across the couch, grabbed my tie, and pulled me to her, our faces inches apart. Just as I was about to deliver the hook line, "We can't do this, I'm your dad's best friend," there was a knock at the front door.

"Cut!" yelled Don, dropping the camera to his side. "Benji, get the door."

Benji took off his headphones and unclipped the audio recorder from his belt, resting it on the couch along with the boom pole. He walked to the front door and opened it. Standing there was Aliya Boujee, the female talent for the next scene. A bay area native, Aliya was a fierce twenty-three-year-old with scattered piercings and a Medusa tattoo on her stomach. Her hair was dyed pink, but her dark roots were showing. She was wearing a Henley crop top, the barbels of her nipple piercings jutting through the thin fabric. Fingernails manicured into sharp claws, one hand was wrapped around an open beer bottle and the other around the handle of her suitcase. There was a freshly rolled blunt tucked behind one ear.

"Boujee's here, bitches," she said, sticking out her tongue and waggling it, a titanium stud clicking against her teeth.

"Shit, you got a beer for me too?" asked Benji.

"Here, finish this," said Aliya, handing him the bottle. "It's nothing but backwash anyway."

"Oh, gee, thanks," he said. Then, calling to Don, "What do you say, beer with lunch?"

Don mulled it over. "Fuck it. It's Friday. Get a case when you pick up the food."

"Oh, and some vodka too," said Aliya.

"Now we're talking," said Benji.

"Whatever she wants," said Don. "Just none of that raspberry crap like last time."

"Yeah, yeah, you know you love it," Aliya said, wheeling her bag to the makeup room.

Benji left to pick up lunch. We prepped to shoot sex stills in his absence. Wendy went to the bathroom to douche, and I popped half a Viagra.

Sex stills is a two-part process. Part one consists of solo photos of the female talent stripping while seductively posing at each passing interval until she's completely naked. We call these "Pretty girls." She gets redressed and then begins part two, miming the plot with the male talent while stripping once again until both are naked and ready for sex. Performers then cycle through two oral positions, three to five sex positions, and then the pop-shot. It's all straightforward. A well-versed team would power through them in ten or fifteen minutes.

We wrapped stills. Wendy ducked into the makeup room for a touchup. Benji returned with a feast of McDonald's, a case of

Modelo, and a handle of Tito's, placing everything on the kitchen island.

Aliya reappeared wearing eye masks, her hair partially teased, the blunt still tucked behind her ear. "Shots! Shots! Shots!" she cheered.

"Ten-minute break and then we're back up for video," said Don.

He and I each grabbed a bottle of beer while Benji poured a round of Tito's for himself and Aliya. I went back to the couch, thumbing through Twitter. Aliya took a few extra swigs from the bottle and washed them down with a beer of her own. Then she came over to join me.

"Looggaaannn," she said, cuddling up. I put my arm around her. "They tell you what happened to me?"

Last time Aliya was with Don, a faulty boom pole came loose. The microphone fell from its cradle and hit her square in the face, sending her to the E.R. for stitches. There were no unions in porn, and we didn't get worker's compensation for on-set accidents. I could all but guarantee Aliya paid for the stitches out of pocket, or, at most, Don paid for them out of his. Either way, it's a shitty deal for everyone.

"But really look," she said, rubbing a small red spot above her right eyebrow. "I'm ugly now, aren't I?"

Honestly, I wouldn't have noticed a damn thing had she not been pointing it out and holding it under a spotlight.

"What!? Come on, you look great, you got nothing to worry about."

"Thank you, Logan," she said, hugging me.

Wendy returned from makeup and Aliya jumped off the couch and ran over to her. "Hey sexy," she said, taking the blunt from her ear. "Let's go out to the pool and get high before you fuck." She then scampered into the kitchen and grabbed the vodka bottle to take with her.

"Leave the bottle," said Don, barely looking up as he adjusted settings on his DSLR.

"Fine, fine," said Aliya, taking a swig. "Greedy bitches."

The girls headed out the sliding glass door to the back patio. Benji jogged after. "Hey ladies, courtesy puff?" He closed the door, and they sparked up. He took a long drag before coming back inside. "It's official," he said, going for his McDonald's. "Someone's gotta keep a leash on that chick."

"And who was just out there smoking weed with her?" said Don.

"You know I'm cool," said Benji. "She's jonesing, that's all I'm saying."

"Keep an eye on her, okay?"

"Aye-aye, captain," he replied with a mouthful of fries.

Gia walked out to the kitchen with her purse. "I'm gonna smoke a cigarette out front."

Another knock at the front door. Gia answered it on her way out. It was the male talent for the second scene, a duffel bag slung around his shoulder. He introduced himself as Rick Swole. I hadn't met him before, but he was tall, buff, and tatted. A thick outline in his grey sweatpants confirmed he was the total package.

Aliya saw him through the sliding door and came running back inside. "Mmm, look at you," she said, going in for a hug and running her hands across his body. "You're gonna be blessed by the Boujee today, baby."

"You guys done smoking?" asked Don. "We're killing time here. Aliya, get back into makeup and let us knock out this scene."

Aliya complied, but not before taking another swig of vodka and yet again trying to take the bottle with her.

"Leave the bottle!" he barked. "Makeup. Now. Go."

"All right, all right, sheeeit," she said, walking off with her male talent in tow.

Wendy came back inside, and Don called to her. "What do you say we make sexy time?"

On *action*, I delivered the hook line. Wendy hopped into my lap and sucked my tongue, while grinding me to dust. The sex was rabid. I barely had enough time to take off my clothes before Wendy flipped upside down and demanded I face-fuck her while stuffing her white panties into her pink pussy. Within minutes her makeup ran, and her fake eyelashes fell off, getting stuck on her spit covered cheeks. I removed the rest of my clothes but kept my tie on at her request. We fucked in missionary, her feet shoved in my mouth; spoon, my hands wrapped around her neck from both sides; doggystyle, up and over, my foot crushing her face into the cushions. She goaded me to use her any way I pleased. Her body was mine. This was her apology for last time, and she was well on her way to forgiveness.

A crash. Glass shattered in the makeup room. A hand mirror had been thrown against a wall. The door swung open, angry foot-steps boomed toward us. A raspy slurred voice shrieked through the hall. "Ya'll better cancel my scene. I ain't got time for this!"

Wendy and I froze mid-stroke to see Aliya foaming at the mouth, eye masks still on and makeup undone. Her left eye twitched as she swayed back and forth, barely able to keep her balance.

"What the fuck?" Don said. "We're in the middle of sex."

"Ya'll ain't even done the first scene and I got places to be," she said. "I ain't got time to wait around and my makeup ain't even done yet." Aliya singled out Benji. "This dumb ass drops some shit on my face last time, and now I got a scar and I'm ugly and I don't wanna fuckin' shoot looking like this!"

"*Aliya*," Don said, trying to remain calm. "We have two positions left and then you're up. What's the problem?"

"If my makeup aint done in ten minutes I'm walkin'," she said.

"Well, why aren't you in the chair? Where's Gia?"

"She hasn't been there! That bitch up and left."

Benji set down his sound equipment and opened the front door, peering toward the driveway. "Her car's gone," he said.

Aliya screamed, "That's what I'm saying—ya'll ain't listen to me!"

"I'll call her," said Don, taking his phone out of his pocket. "Aliya, please just go into the makeup room and wait so we can finish shooting."

"No!" she screamed. "I'm sick of you bitch-asses. I've been talking to a lawyer, I'm 'bout to sue you—look at my fucking face! I got 8k in my bank account, ya'll think I'm playing? I'm Aliya fuckin' Boujee. Ya'll think I need to shoot porn? Nah, I got 50k in my bank account. Try me, bitch!"

Wendy and I untangled ourselves. Still naked, we escaped the crossfire, walking out to the patio. I sat on a lounge chair while she anxiously paced the perimeter of the in-ground pool.

"My nerves are like going crazy right now," she said. "I knew something like this would happen. While we were smoking, she was talking so much trash about everyone. She's two-faced."

"She's drunk," I said, loosening my tie.

Through the sliding glass door, I saw Aliya was now on the phone. I could hear her muffled yelling. "You have to come get me," she said. "It's the same loser crew that fucked up my face. Come inside if you have to, just get here!"

Wendy looked shaken. "That's not good," she said. "You heard what her last boyfriend did, right? He fucking killed someone."

"What!?" I said, the hairs on my neck standing up.

"Yeah, she was fighting with some dude at a party, and her boyfriend took out a gun and fucking shot him. My heart is, like, racing," she said, putting a hand to her chest.

I was feeling a little uneasy too with that newfound information. I slipped back indoors, and without calling too much attention to myself, I put my clothes back on and started packing my stuff. Benji sat at the kitchen island, earbuds in, watching Youtube while finishing his McDonalds. I eavesdropped as Don and Aliya continued to argue.

"Gia is on her way back," he said. "She left because her son got a concussion. The principal of his school called and said he got hit in the head and she needed to come get him."

Aliya roared back, "I GOT HIT IN THE HEAD AND YA'LL AIN'T DO SHIT. FUCK THAT KID!"

"Aliya! He's eight-years-old!"

"I don't give a fuck about her bitch-ass kid. I want my booking back!"

"What booking?"

"Today, motherfucker!"

"Let me get this straight," Don said. "You show up drinking, get wasted, interrupt the scene before you, threaten us, and now you want us to rebook you!?"

Aliya started to cry. "I don't need to do this shit!"

"Which is it? Do you or do you not want to shoot?"

"I want my bookings!"

"Jesus *fucking* Christ," he said, resigned.

I headed toward the front door with my stuff.

"And where the hell are you going?" Don called out.

"Look," I said, approaching him and keeping my voice low. "I'm getting my shit situated in case some dude rushes in here and all hell breaks loose. No way am I sticking around for that—I'm male talent, boyfriends hate me. Even if I'm not the one fucking her, I'm the enemy by default."

"All right, all right, just hurry back," he said.

I brought my bags to the car, tossed them in the backseat. Leaning against the door, I debated whether I should bother going back in at all or if I should just jump in the car and get out of there while I had the chance. Go AWOL. Drive until the wheels fell off. Start over in a new city under a false name.

I imagined how the crime scene photos would look if I stayed and someone did open fire. A body slouched over a case of beer. Another with a half-eaten hamburger in his mouth. Blood sprayed across the walls like an amateur Jackson Pollock. Camera lenses and light bulbs smashed into a million pieces, shards of glass sparkling across the tile floor. Shot through bottles of lube oozing their slimy contents. Wendy and I riddled with holes, our bodies still intertwined, the two of us framed as ill-fated lovers instead of the relative strangers we were. I could see the newspaper headlines. "Horror in the Valley," they'd read. "Porn Stars Killed in a Hail of Gunfire."

Thoughts of that crime scene got me thinking about another—Venus and her bloodshot eyes, skyward boots in the background. All it took was a little free association and suddenly I was back in my bathroom naked with a full bladder and a hard-on wondering what the fuck just happened. I hadn't thought about her in months. Some part of me wanted to know if what I saw was true. I checked her socials. Still inactive except for more automated tweets. I logged into Skype. Unsurprisingly, she wasn't online. I typed a message anyway, doing my best to appear discreet in the off chance her account was being monitored by someone other than her.

"Hey, long time no see," I said. "What's new? Catch me up. Please call me when you see this. Would love to talk. Anytime."

Just then, Aliya was being escorted out by Don. I considered ducking out of her line of sight, worried she'd continue her tirade in the driveway, but it seemed a switch had been flipped. She was now as docile as an apologetic puppy.

She saw me. "Looggann," she called out, her voice deflated. I pursed my lips in an awkward smile and walked toward her. She went in for a hug. "I'm sorry for ruining your scene," she said.

"It's whatever," I said, weakly returning the gesture. I broke away and headed back inside.

Rick Swole was nursing a beer in the kitchen, duffel bag at his feet. "I guess this means I got the day to myself then."

"Looks like it," I said.

A few minutes later, Don came through the front door. "The bitch is gone!" he said. "Pour me a shot!"

Benji filled a glass and Don slugged it, slamming it down on the countertop. "Now, who's ready to fuck?"

ELEVEN

I was supposed to be in the air on my way to Vegas for two days of work, but LAX was in turmoil.

Flights were being delayed and then re-routed to different terminals as a constant tide of irate commuters hauled their luggage back and forth. To make matters worse, I ate the rest of the peach weed gummies—120 mg in total—before leaving my apartment, and it was now hitting me all at once. My tongue was sandpaper, my throat closed in, eyes so dry I couldn't open them beyond a squint under the oppressive airport fluorescents. Fear and paranoia grew. Was I drawing too much attention? Did I look suspicious? I found a vacant gate and quickly took a seat to calm myself. I was nervous to move, afraid I would somehow be scolded if I looked at anyone the wrong way. I shrunk into myself, regressing into a scared little boy. Through my haze, I spotted a storefront housing a wall of refrigerators stocked with ice cold water bottles. Salvation. I worked up the courage to venture over and buy two, immediately chugging one over a trashcan and dumping the empty shell when I was finished. I could swallow again, no longer lost in the desert, but I was still stranded in the airport.

I found my actual gate and figured I'd kill time by watching a movie. I took out my laptop and pressed the power button. No go. The battery was dead. I dug through my carry-on for the charger and then wandered around like the walking dead looking for an outlet to plug into. I found one and tried to stick in the prongs, only for them to bounce back. I tried again, and same thing. Once more, this time slow and determined, but the prongs still wouldn't fit. It was then I realized this wasn't an outlet at all but a sticker of an outlet someone had stuck on the wall to fool idiots like me. I looked around to see if anyone had noticed, but thankfully everyone else was preoccupied with their own airport struggles.

I packed up my laptop and charger in frustration, then grabbed a double espresso from Starbucks to bring me back to life. As I drank, my senses sharpened and the intense high subsided, the combination of weed and caffeine created a perfectly mellow sensation. I was back in control.

Soon enough, my flight boarded. I shuffled with the rest of the passengers in a slow line down the jetway, nodding to the Southwest flight crew as I stepped onto the plane. There was an open seating policy, so I surveyed my options. I'd heard the area around the wings was usually the most reinforced, and therefore the safest place to be in case the bird went down. I found a window seat in the emergency row on top of the left wing. I sat and cracked open my second water bottle, taking a few sips before placing it in the netted pocket. An attendant came over to confirm my competency in operating the window latch in the unlikely case of an emergency. I gave her a thumbs up and then put in my ear buds, cranking the volume. I closed my eyes and slowed my breathing, the poor man's speedball from earlier assuaging my worries as we taxied to the runway.

Ten minutes later we were wheels up and approaching cruising altitude. I released my death grip from the arms of my seat. Drink orders were taken. The water vibrated calmy in the bottle. All was well.

A loud thud came from the rear of the plane. As we all took a second to look back, the cabin lights flickered, stealing our attention. "Someone must've forgotten to pay the electric bill," a flight attendant joked. Another thud, this time accompanied by rumbling. The water bottle slipped from the net and onto the floor. As I reached down to pick it up, the cabin started shaking violently as if tearing itself apart. Overhead bins flung open, and luggage toppled out. Flight attendants were attempting to calm the passengers when we suddenly dove forward, sending the water bottle and every other fucking thing not nailed down hurtling toward the cockpit door. Oxygen masks dropped from the ceiling, and everyone instinctively grabbed theirs. Everyone but me. Running on pure adrenaline, I ripped my tray table from the seat in front of me. Then I yanked the latch for the emergency window, the rupture causing a massive tear in the fuselage. I unbuckled my seatbelt, mounted my feet on the tray table, and took a leap of faith, sailing through the sky like the Silver Surfer, toward an oncoming mountain range. I landed with superhuman grace, riding my tray down the steep cliffside. The plane crashed and burned behind me sending an avalanche of twisted metal and debris my way as I raced to the bottom. A butterscotch blonde was waiting for me there in the passenger seat of a candy red topless Porsche 911. I ditched the tray and hopped in, hitting the gas as she attacked my zipper. The two of us hightailed it out of there toward the horizon and an uncertain future filled with unlimited possibilities.

Ding!

The fasten seatbelt sign. My eyes cracked open. I was still seated on the plane, my headphones dangling from my shirt collar. The water bottle secured in front of me, its contents rhythmically swaying. There was no thud, no loss of cabin pressure. I had fallen asleep on what was just another routine flight, and we were now making our final descent toward Las Vegas.

Safely on the ground I grabbed my checked bag and exited the arrivals terminal. Stepping outside of the temperature-controlled airport was like sticking my face in an oven, the summer heat so thick I had to wade through it. I walked to the rideshare pickup zone and caught a car to the shoot house in the supposed "Arts

District" just north of the strip.

For both days of production, all the talent stayed together in a loft apartment, which also served as our set. There with me was Lana Luv, Kody Sly, and Billy Cedar. Lana Luv was a MILF from the Midwest who entered the business following a messy divorce. A former evangelical, Lana now unabashedly fulfilled her fantasies on camera. Kody Sly was a budding starlet. Standing barely five feet tall and weighing under 100 lbs, she was the definitive spinner. No stranger to rough sex, Kody once tweeted, "Never ask me to change positions, just toss me where you want me." Billy Cedar was a 6'4" hulking Australian footballer, a popular male performer and multi-AVN award winner. Supervising us all for the duration was director Pete Wood, a burnt-out lifer in the business with a potbelly and a gambling addiction. He rocked thick Elvis Presley sideburns and a wiry salt and pepper soul patch on his chin.

After a hard day of playing Lana Luv's horny stepson, I found myself gazing at the skyline on the apartment balcony with Billy Cedar. The immediate view was mostly obstructed by an above-ground parking garage, but I could still make out the needlepoint of the Stratosphere Hotel and the low amber glow of the Circus Circus Casino. Sharing a joint, Billy talked about his life growing up in Australia. In his late teens, he was on track to play soccer professionally, but his knee gave out during a match and he missed his window. Billy completed rehab and after relentless training he earned another offer, this time to play for a Cairo team under the strict condition that he live in Egypt indefinitely. He travelled there and spent a few weeks considering the offer, ultimately declining on account of there being not enough women around.

"Mate, I got fucking problems," he said. "My girlfriend says I'm a sex addict—yeah, no fuckin shit, dummy. How you reckon I ended up in this job?"

"We all got the bug," I said. "You still play soccer, at least?"

"Oh yeah," he said. "I'm captain of a local team in L.A., The Hollywood All Stars. You know of Vinnie Jones?"

"The actor?"

"He owns the team."

"No shit? And you're the captain? So, you're like, the leader, huh?"

"Eh, more like the bully on the field. I watch the team's back; make sure nobody fucks with my mates."

"Right on."

"So," Billy said, taking a puff, "I hear you're having a bout with Magnus."

"Milo?" I said. "How'd you know that?"

"C'mon, mate, everyone talks in this business. 'Specially him. You want my advice?"

"Please."

"You gotta apologize."

"Apologize?" I said. "For what? I didn't do anything."

"It don't matter. Milo's a real cunt, everything's always a pissing contest. All you gotta do is make him feel like he's won and he'll drop it."

"I'll think about it. Thanks."

The next morning, I woke to a DM from Kody Sly, my intended partner for the day. "Hey dude," she said. "I think I have a yeast infection or something so probably don't eat me out today. Also I might've torn yesterday cuz I'm spotting. It's cool though."

I didn't respond. This is where the testing falls short; anything can happen in that fourteen-day window. I might be clean today but tomorrow was anyone's guess. My mind drifted in the worst direction. All I imagined were the possible STDs I could catch. The oozing drip, swollen nodes. The work I'd have to cancel, and the money I'd lose.

It's cool though.

By the time I got dressed I was fuming. I went looking for Pete and found him in the living room on the couch playing poker on his phone, a camo flat brim with the word PORN emblazoned across it sat lopsided on his head. Billy was next to him drinking a breakfast beer. Across the room Kody was on a bar stool in the kitchen having her lips done by the makeup artist, Alice. Lana was pouring herself a cup of coffee. My judgement was clouded, and instead of taking Pete aside and handling the situation in private, I decided to air out my dirty laundry right there.

"I don't feel safe working with Kody," I said, everyone's ears perking. "I want to switch scene partners."

"You're kidding, right?" said Pete. "The fuck?"

"She said some shit to me that's got me concerned. It's my right to speak up if I don't feel comfortable, so that's what I'm doing."

Billy stood up next to me and patted me on the shoulder. "Good on you, mate," he said. "I'll take Kody again, I don't mind."

Pete burped. "Fine. Whatever. You're up first then, Billy."

Once Kody was out of makeup, she and Billy went into one of the bedrooms and shot their scene with Pete behind the camera. Alice started on Lana's makeup. The air in the room was tense. I went outside to the balcony and kept to myself. I knew I was an asshole to embarrass Kody like that. While the outcome might've been the same, I could have at least used some tact and kept it discreet. I also thought about Billy. He was a true workhorse, ready and willing to do the job at hand, no questions asked. I admired him.

Two hours later, it was time for Lana and me. She went to the bathroom to douche, and I walked into the bedroom with Pete. He closed the door behind us.

"What was that shit about?" he said, nearly backing me into a wall. "Who do you think you are? You can't just change partners because you don't want to fuck the bitch you're paired with. You're lucky Billy is here to pick up the pieces. He's the real deal, not some closet twink like you."

"Look, you don't understand." I started.

"No, you don't understand, fucko," he said, cutting me off. "You're not in charge. We'll shoot this scene and then you're never coming back here, got it?"

"Are you serious?"

"Dead fucking serious," he said, eyes locked. "Try me."

My stare wavered. I cowered. "...Got it," was all I could manage. By this point, I didn't want to fuck, I just wanted to go home.

We shot the scene, but it wasn't pretty. Even with the power of the pill, I had trouble controlling my blood flow. If that wasn't bad enough, during the popshot, the unthinkable happened. From a deep throat position, Lana milked me into her mouth as intended, but her gag reflex caused her to accidentally swallow the entire lot before the camera saw any of it. The pop-shot today was paramount. So important, in fact, Pete was unwilling to fake it. He demanded I work up another.

"And make it quick," he said. "I don't want to waste my whole day with this bullshit."

TWELVE

I slept through my alarm. When I saw the clock, I shot up in a panic. My call time was in twenty minutes, and it was an hour-long commute. I got my shit together, had a quick shower, and hit the road. I texted the director. He responded with an enthusiastic, "K." If there's one thing directors are sticklers about, it's talent showing up on time, even with the trending motto: "Hurry up and wait."

Hair wet and stomach empty, I tried in vain to weave through traffic; the morning rush was too heavy. I had no choice but to sit in it and suffer with the rest of the stiffs, watching the minutes drag, each one a reflection of my waning work ethic. Anxious and pissed off, I punched the steering wheel. This was not how I wanted to start the day.

I calmed down by reminding myself I had someone very special waiting for me. I was booked with the illustrious Chloe Creed. With over a dozen awards to her name and top placements in every major publication's "Best of" list, Chloe was easily one of the most popular girls in porn.

On set, Chloe was all smiles. Wearing only white tennis shoes and tube socks, she danced around the house while the director followed close behind with his camera. "I'm here to do two things," she said into the lens. "Make people laugh and give guys boners." With an attitude like that it was easy to see how she'd become such a fan favourite.

I filled out my paperwork, popped my pill, and it was time to get to work. We started with stills, first of us kissing and then of Chloe lounging back on a chaise longue as I went down on her. I took my time, enjoying the taste even after the director said he had enough pictures. "Okay, stud," he said. "You can eat it all you want on video. Next position."

I took Chloe's seat and she dropped to her knees. I was ready to relax and have the earlier stress of the morning melt away.

Just as Chloe was about to wrap her lips around me, she paused and softly said, "Um, can we cut, please?"

The director lowered the camera.

"What's up?" I asked.

"There's a weird looking sore here," she said. "Like the skin isn't broken but it looks pretty raw."

"Oh my god, really?"

"Yeah. I think we might want to hold off."

I looked at it, and sure enough she was right, I had a patch of inflamed skin on the underside of my shaft—the early sign of another herpes outbreak.

We cancelled the scene and made a rain check for some undetermined date. I went home empty-handed. With a girl as busy as Chloe, booking her required scheduling months in advance, and because of her high profile, having her on set meant producers were shelling out more cash than for an average performer. So, we postponed, but that was a nice way of the director saying I blew it, and the opportunity to work with Chloe was lost. Sure, they might have been able to rebook her, but what were the odds they'd hire me back and risk the same thing happening again? Zero. Which is exactly what I felt like that day, a big fucking zero. No sex, no money, no prospects.

As shitty as it was to force another cancellation, nothing could excuse the fact that I almost exposed my partner to herpes. Even if I was unaware of it at the time, who's to say I didn't knowingly show up with visible sores? Maybe she already caught it or maybe she didn't, but either way I couldn't afford to be known as the dipshit who came to work sick. Something like that was unforgivable. Forget being No-listed by Malibu Models, I'd be cast into industry exile.

These outbreaks were becoming more frequent and appearing with less warning as the days went on. All it would take was a little stress and a slight rattling of my cage for my unwanted houseguests to make their return. Even with supplementing my medication twice a day and triple dosing on Lysine, they were still always there, festering below the surface of my skin, appearing at will and sending me on a downward spiral of self-pity, loathing, and disgust. I hated them and I hated myself for being a host to this demon.

Overdramatic? Sure. Herpes is unsightly, it's contagious, and it made me feel dirty, but if I didn't rely on my dick to make a living, it really wouldn't be much more than an annoyance. Millions of people each year are diagnosed, and they go on with their lives seemingly unaffected 99% of the time. They find ways to cope and learn to avoid triggers, they make plans and contingencies. All things I'd have to discover sooner or later. But the fact would remain: I was infected, and it would follow me forever.

More time off meant more time to consider my future in this business and my place in the food chain. If I wanted to have a chance at turning things around for myself, I'd have to do my part to maintain a good rapport with those in charge.

I thought about the conversation I had with Billy on the balcony. Milo Magnus and his petty grievances. Agents were necessary evils in this business, sometimes just as important as producers when it came to getting that call to work. As much as I'd come to dislike him, I figured it was time for me to reach out to Milo and apologize—for what, I didn't have the slightest, but I was going to do my best to play nice and make amends.

I googled Malibu Models, found the office number, and dialed. As the phone rang, my index finger on my free hand picked at the cuticles of my thumb.

A woman answered. "Malibu Models," she said. "How may I direct your call?"

"Logan Pierce calling for Milo Magnus," I said.

"Logan Pierce?"

"Correct, calling for Milo."

"One moment, please," she said, putting me on hold.

One moment turned into one minute, which stretched into three. I had half a mind to hang up, but then I heard a click on the other line.

"Yes?" a nasally voice said. It was Milo.

"Hi," I said. "This is Logan Pierce."

No reply.

"Hello? Milo?"

"Yes," he said, agitated as if a simple hello was beneath him.

"Yeah, hi, this is Logan Pierce, like I said, uh, just hoping to talk to you for a minute about, you know, the situation that happened in Vegas."

"Do you have something you'd like to say?" he said as if urging an insubordinate child. I wouldn't let him get to me, though. I kept my cool.

"Well, that whole mess was a complete misunderstanding," I said. "And I just want you to know that I take full responsibility for it, and I apologize."

"I see. And what exactly are you apologizing for?"

"For, um, inconveniencing your model and causing the shoot to be cancelled, I guess."

"You *guess?*" he said. "Doesn't sound very sincere, now does it, Logan?"

"*Milo,*" I said, my cool slipping. "I said I was sorry. I just want us to be able to move on."

"Why?" he asked. "You not booking enough work these days? Worried more people might No-list you?"

"This doesn't have to be personal. I don't understand the point of us being enemies. We can both make money together, doesn't that make the most sense?"

"...No, I don't think so."

"Why not?"

"Who's to say you won't do it again?"

"Do what?!" I said, my vision turning red. "What did I do besides follow the rules? Honestly, I don't even know what you want me to apologize for."

"I've gathered as much," he said. "Logan, you wasted my girl's time. She lost work, which meant I didn't get paid."

"Fine. I understand that. I lost work that day too. And then we rescheduled, and you deliberately waited until after I flew in to cancel it. How is that not worse?"

"You needed to be taught a lesson. Do not fuck with another man's money."

"And you taught me that by fucking with my money? Brilliant. Lesson learned."

"No, I don't think so," he said. "Tell you what, I'll take you off the list. For a price. My girl's rate."

"You want me to pay you?"

"Twelve-hundred dollars, Logan. That's the offer. Take it or leave it."

"Unbelievable. You really are a piece of work, you know that?"

"Resorting to name calling, are we? Well then, you've made your choice. No-listed you shall remain. I don't think we have anything further to discuss. Best of luck with your so-called career." The line disconnected.

"Mother Fucker!" I threw my phone against the couch. The attempted truce backfired and left me with nothing but egg on my face. There would be no peace. Whatever. I didn't need his approval. Fuck him.

THIRTEEN

A few days passed. The sores cleared up and I got a fresh test. Beverly had texted with a job offer. Brazzers wanted me in Vegas. B/B/G/G for $600. I wasn't usually one for group activities: my first gangbang had left me double dosed on Viagra, dizzy and wide eyed as I stared at a feeding frenzy. I'd avoided them ever since. The price tag was appealing, though. I asked who the other guy was. Billy Cedar. It'd be nice to catch up. Plus, I figured I owed him one for the last time. He'd make a great tag-team partner. Rock and Roll.

Five A.M. Morning of. I revived under a steaming shower. I got dressed, packed up, and caught a car to the airport. I checked my bag and shuffled through security. Walking to my terminal, I saw Billy across the way at a bar. He was sipping a beer and watching ESPN on the TV.

I patted his shoulder. "Morning, Captain."

He turned. A sincere smile. "Ah, mornin', mate." He tipped his glass toward me. "Heart-starter for brekkie?"

The bartender walked over. "Get you anything?"

Fuck it. "Modelo," I said.

"That's the spirit," said Billy.

My beer came. Billy grabbed his. "Hold yours out," he said. I did and he lifted his glass above mine. "Maybe above ya." He moved his glass below mine. "Maybe below ya." He moved his glass level with mine. "But always beside ya." He cheered and we clinked glasses. Nothing like the taste of toothpaste and cerveza first thing in the morning.

"Took your advice," I said. "Apologized to Milo."

"And?"

"A total wash. I think I even somehow made it worse. Says the only way off the No-list is to pay him."

"How much?"

"Twelve hundred."

"Fuck me dead, mate. Sorry 'bout that."

"Can't win 'em all, I guess."

"Least you tried."

"Least I tried."

We finished the beers and boarded our flight. I slept the entire hour. No need for the water bottle trick today.

In Vegas, Brazzers had Billy and I playing home security installers assigned to the house of two voluptuous MILFs, both blonde, bronze, and filled to the brim with plastic. The two of them were dressed in very bright and very tight athletic wear, on their way to the gym, giving us unfettered access to their home. Billy and I took advantage of their absence, snooping around and prying through their cabinets and closets. In the bedroom we found vibrators in the nightstands and rifled through panty drawers, gathering handfuls to sniff, stuffing our favourites into our pockets. We installed the cameras the women wanted but also placed a hidden pinhole camera in the bathroom pointed directly at the shower. When our work was done, we drove our company van around the corner to wait. Soon the women returned, sweaty and desperate for a rinse. They both entered the bathroom and seductively stripped in front of our hidden camera, Billy and I practically creamed at the visuals, howling in as the women stepped into the shower and bathed each other, soapy tits pressed against the glass as if putting on a show in our honour. Suddenly, the hidden camera fell loose, falling to the ground. Overcome with horny delirium, we decided to sneak into the house and fix it before the women could notice. Crawling on all fours, we reached the camera the exact moment they turned off the water and stepped out, discovering us and our crimes. Our eyes locked, and we all screamed and pulled exaggerated shock faces in classic Brazzers fashion. Dripping wet, the women gave us an ultimatum: either they call the cops, or we strip down and fuck them right then and there. *Porno logic.*

I popped my half a pill, and it was time for stills. Billy and I stood side by side, him a foot taller. The women knelt before us. Billy pulled out his cock. It was a sword, razor sharp, curving straight up in the air. I followed suit. Half-mast and gummy. I started stroking. The girls attacked Billy, flanking him from either side, one on the shaft, the other on ball duty. The photographer snapped photos of them. I took a step outside of the frame. The women lifted Billy's shirt. A tanned six-pack underneath. He was hard everywhere. I worked up a good enough edge and walked back in, just in time for the photographer to announce, "Enough BJ, move on to sex." The women laid on their backs, side by side and legs spread on top of the oversized bathroom countertop. Billy and I approached. He was so tall he had to kneel to reach his partner, fists so large they wrapped fully around her ankles. On tippy toes, my cock barely reached over the counter. The crew brought in the apple box. *Kill me now.*

I excused myself to go to the actual bathroom, grabbing my pants on the way. I dug through my front pocket and found the other half of Viagra. I had no time to wait for it to break down in my stomach; I used a soap dish to crush the pill into a powder, then stuck my finger in it and rubbed it all into my gums. Returning to set, Billy was fucking one of the women in cowgirl while the other sat on his face, both making out above him. My presence was immediately felt. The mood dropped. The woman on his face crawled off and got on all fours, facing away from me. I did my best, but my wood was up and down. The photographer tried to incorporate me, but most of the shots ended up focused on Billy and the women. Every time I stopped to fluff myself, my partner would lean over and join the happy couple. I didn't blame her.

Stills took nearly an hour to shoot. I doubt there was even a single photo where I was hard. I was so frustrated, by the time we were done, I was on the verge of tears. I ducked away back into the other bathroom to beat myself up in the mirror—*You're embarrassing yourself out there, you limp dick loser.* My eyes watered. Had it really come to this? Was my ego so fragile, self-esteem so low, all it took was a soft cock to make me cry?

A knock at the door. "Hey, mate."

I cracked it open and stuck my head out. Billy was there. Had he come to check on me? To give me a pep-talk? My hero. He was wrapped in a towel, his muscles shiny, figure strong and eyes tender. Fuck him for looking so good. "What's up," he said. "You all right?"

"Um, yeah I guess so," I said, my chin quivering. "Just having an off day. I swear this never happens to me." The earlier words of Wendy Waves were now flowing from my mouth. How easy it was to find myself on this side of that conversation.

"Reckon you want a pill or something?" he said.

"That's the thing, I already took a whole Viagra. I don't know where my head's at."

"Oh," he said. "Well, you ever think about shooting up? You know, as a sort of backup for these things."

I thought about what it meant to shoot up. Much like the pills, injecting is another form of artificial stimulation. It's a liquid compound loaded into a syringe and jabbed into the spongy corpus cavernosum of the penis. A lot of guys in porn do it, but it's not openly talked about. It's easy to spot if you know what you're looking for: dicks swollen like overfilled water balloons. The obvious tell is a small red dot or bruise near the base of the shaft indicating the puncture site. Unlike pills, which could have a delayed reaction or no reaction at all, injecting produces near immediate results, and the effects can last a couple hours. It's clear why some preferred it. I'd be lying if I said I wasn't at least a little curious to experience that power. Only problem, it's easy to overdose. I'd heard rumours of a guy who shot up, his dick becoming so bloated he couldn't touch it without wincing, couldn't walk without doubling over. Supposedly there was so much blood in his shaft that his skin turned purple. He'd ended up in the emergency room where hospital staff stuck more needles in his dick, this time to drain it before the surging blood left him permanently impotent. No thank you.

"Is that what you do?" I asked Billy.

"Hell nah, mate," he said. "That shit'll fuck you up proper. I sell it, though, if you ever want it."

"Good to know."

"I'm just right fucked in the head," he continued. "The wind keeps me hard most days."

The director called for us. It was time for video.

Billy patted me on the shoulder. "Don't beat yourself up, mate," he said. "You're a stud. Now let's have some fun and fuck these chicks."

On *action*, Billy took center stage, handling both women with ease, putting on a show, selling his performance. I slid my pants down and was soft—the worst place a male performer could find himself in during video. Growing in real time. A defining moment separating pros from the mopes. I was the only thing that stood between a finished product and a total loss. I didn't want to go out like a loser, unable to finish the job, forced to go home again with my tail between my legs. I was only as good as my last scene. I pressed on, utilizing softcore tricks to hide my fluctuating wood. A doggy position with one of the women, her face toward the camera, me humping from behind, sometimes inside, other times flapping against the back of her thighs. I spent an unreasonable amount of time sucking titties and eating pussy, my arm furiously tugging just off camera.

While Billy provided 95% of the hardcore, the director still insisted on having shots of me in action. I knew he was unhappy, but he maintained his cool and made me a compromise. He only needed five minutes of solid penetration before we could set up the pop. A fair deal. I dug deep, closing my eyes, and focusing on every seedy and perverted act I could think of, recalling scenes of my favourite old school performers done up like perfect fuck dolls spewing obscenities at the camera while being railed into oblivion. I prayed to the porn gods, and this time they listened. I found a rhythm and kept up through the entire five minutes, even having enough momentum to propel the pop shot. The women applauded after I came. Patronizing, sure, but I was just happy to have made it out the other side alive.

FOURTEEN

Fall had arrived, but you wouldn't know it by the weather. The only indication was the sudden appearance of Halloween decorations outside people's homes, and in bars and restaurants. It was October 17th—my birthday. My parents called in the morning to wish me a good one and tell me they loved me and missed me. My phone buzzed every few minutes with happy birthday notifications. Otherwise, it was business as usual.

I flew back to Vegas for work, this time for the company Glamour Girls, which specialized in vanilla lovemaking. Sex was sensual and the lighting soft. Penetration shots were unnecessary, the primary focus being authentic chemistry between partners.

They paired me with one of my personal favourites, Aubrey Starflower. When Aubrey had entered the business the previous year, I had the distinction of being her first on-screen partner. Straight out of the gate, Aubrey hit her marks, knew every position, and assumed them all as if she had been bred for this job. I wanted a million copies of her in the bedroom. Even as a first timer, it was clear Aubrey was going to become a force in the industry. She commanded the room, and not in a try-hard way like some other wannabes. Aubrey's allure was effortless and pulled everyone in like gravity.

The scene in Vegas was phenomenal. We fit together like puzzle pieces. Aubrey submitted her body and brought out something visceral in me: no thoughts, only instinct. My purpose was to satisfy, fulfill. The cameras disappeared. I was overdue for something like this, a reminder why I loved this job. Ask me about the best scenes of my career and this one would come damn near close to the top of the list. A happy birthday to me, indeed.

An hour later Aubrey and I were showered, dressed, packed, and paid. The crew had all gone home, leaving the two of us alone to occupy ourselves until our airport shuttle arrived. In the living room, Aubrey lounged on the couch, her head resting on the middle cushions and her feet dangling over the armrest. She idled on her phone while King Harvest's "Dancing in the Moonlight" played from its speakers. I joined her, mirroring her position, the crowns of our heads barely touching. I closed my eyes, visions of our sex replaying in my mind: Aubrey holding me by the shaft, staring at it and saying in earnest, "This might be the most beautiful cock ever." I don't know if she was trying to make me fall in love, but it was working. I nodded off as the daydream lulled me to sleep.

I woke to the sound of Aubrey slamming the bathroom door. I could hear her crying on the phone. I knew it was none of my business but I was curious, so I put my ear to the door. I learned that one of her oldest friends, Tyler, had just died by suicide and I heard her confess that she had been avoiding his calls the past few weeks.

That's a helpless place: not having taken the time to listen and as a consequence having to live with regret over something that couldn't be changed.

I went back to the living room and a few minutes later Aubrey emerged, wiping the bleeding mascara from her face. In a trance, she collected her things; our airport shuttle was on its way. She barely had one shoe on when she burst into tears and crumbled to the floor. I approached her but couldn't think of anything to say so I did the only thing I could think of: I put my arms around her. She reached out and squeezed me tight, crying on my shoulder. I rubbed her back, remaining silent but present, offering comfort through contact.

Aubrey composed herself and we climbed into the shuttle, keeping discussion topics light, doing our best to remain upbeat. I sent her a few funny GIFs and memes that made her smile in the moment.

"Thank you, Logan," she said, head resting on my shoulder.

We were flying Southwest. After checking in we discovered we were in the last boarding group, so by the time we got on the plane, only the middle seats remained and we had to sit apart. After we landed, I saw Aubrey rush off the plane. I could've caught up to say goodbye, but it seemed inconsequential. She had more important things to worry about. Naïvely, I figured I'd probably see her again in a few weeks and she'd be back to her bubbly self.

As I later learned, Tyler's death was just the beginning of heartbreak for Aubrey. After burying her friend, she learned her boyfriend of three years had been cheating on her. She dumped him, and as a final act of humiliation he sent photos and videos of her scenes to all of her relatives on Facebook: aunts, uncles, grandparents. People who could barely navigate social media were now suddenly bombarded with explicit clips of their loved one's gangbang. Aubrey's shitty ex even sent photos to her relative's friends—anyone and everyone who could've possibly been unaware of Aubrey's career. Then came the cyber-bullying—vile comments from strangers and old acquaintances. "A disgrace to your family." "Rot in Hell." "Kill Yourself." Some of her family members quit their jobs. Aubrey's teenage cousins even started getting harassed at school. As a result, Aubrey was ostracized by her family.

What happened next came as a gut punch and took the air out of everyone. Tragically, it's not an uncommon occurrence in this business. One early November morning, a neighbour called 911 and reported a body hanging from a tree in a small park in Encino. It was Aubrey.

If I could go back to that night at the airport, I like to think I would have made more of an effort to find her, to hold her one last time and say goodbye. But that's self-serving, something to make me feel significant. The truth is, there's nothing I could've said or done that would've made any difference. I didn't know Aubrey. At best I experienced a snapshot of her. We were intimate but we weren't close. I never even learned her real name.

FIFTEEN

I was at a house party in the Hills, drinking, smoking, and snorting like there was no tomorrow. All I had was now, living for the moment before I withered away and turned to dust. At least, that's what I was telling myself. I could have used my time to do something meaningful like get an education, volunteer at homeless shelters, or strike a match and set the world on fire. Instead, I used it to wallow and get fucked up.

I was getting sweet with some chick who came out of nowhere and stuck her tongue in my mouth before reaching for my belt. We must've fucked on camera before, because no civilian I'd ever met would just start giving a blowjob in the middle of a party, but there we were, me pulling down my pants and her kneeling so she could do what she did best. I couldn't see straight, but thank God my dick still worked. A crowd formed around us, cheering and taking videos on their phones. The bright flashes casted us under a spotlight. In control, I cupped the back of her head and forced myself further down her throat, hips thrusting in her face. Suddenly I went numb, lightheaded. Her mouth was warm, but I felt nothing. Then I noticed the smell of iron. The party fell silent. The lights and cameras burned. I looked down. She looked back at me, smiling, her face caked red. In one hand was a blade, in the other was my severed flesh, shrivelling as it deflated. Blood spurted down my legs and pooled around me, yet I felt no pain. Slowly, I extended my hand toward the crowd. They parted to allow one of their own through to present a small pillow. Resting on top was a pearl handled .38. Immaculate. I wondered why I hadn't thought of it before, why it took total castration for me to finally work up the nerve. My fingers wrapped around the handle, its girth familiar, its weight intimidating. I pulled back the hammer and put the barrel in my mouth.

BANG!

My eyes burst open. I fought for air, my body drenched in a cold sweat. I caught my breath and realized where I was as my eyes adjusted to the darkness: alone in bed. I reached down to find I was still intact. The moon illuminated my skin. No blood.

I stumbled into the bathroom and splashed cold water on my face, scrubbing my skin. I shook my head, trying to knock the nightmare loose from my brain. Flicking on the light, I stared at my reflection in the speckled mirror of the medicine cabinet. Tan skin and dead eyes looked back: a pretty, hollow shell. I hardly recognized myself.

I guess when one's worth is measured in pop-shots it's bound to lead to a distorted self-image.

SIXTEEN

I was settling down with my morning coffee and scrolling through Twitter when I got a call from Beverly.

"Bad news, sweetie," she said. "I know this wasn't your Christmas wish, but I need you to clear your calendar. Cancel everything this week and put the rest of the month on hold. A moratorium has been called."

"What's a moratorium?"

"It's when the entire industry shuts down production."

"But why would it shut down?"

"Someone tested positive for HIV."

"...Fuck." First Aubrey, now this.

"I'll call you once I find out more," she said. "And sweetie, don't freak out or nothing, but you need to get retested. Your name was flagged, and you're on the list."

"The list?"

"The first-generation list. You may have worked with the person who tested positive."

The colour left my face. "I *may* have?"

"They never tell us who tested positive. Violation of privacy and all that. They just call the agencies if one of our talents need to come in. Like I said, don't freak out, just get your ass over to Talent HQ."

My hands were shaking. I needed something to calm me down. I cashed a bowl. Bad idea. The weed made me anxious and paranoid. Head spinning, I rushed over to Talent HQ. The office was solemn. They knew what had happened and why I was there. I peed in a cup, gave my blood. One performer panel: a hundred sixty-five bucks. I went back to my car and stared at the steering wheel. This could be it, I thought. The beginning of the end. I turned the key and left the radio untouched, driving home in silence.

Things were coming apart fast. If I was sick, what was I supposed to do? I was a college dropout living hand-to-mouth. There were no other jobs I could get that would offer me the same freedom. I only had to work for a few hours a couple days a week. Off time was spent at beaches, in bars, partying with friends or eating mushrooms on a Tuesday and wandering around Hollywood Boulevard. I wasn't on anybody's clock but my own. Even with my low rates, I was still paid more for a single day than most people make in a week. So what if I couldn't save a dime? Money was never my goal. There was no endgame for me, no ulterior motive, no backup plan. I got into porn simply because I wanted to fuck on camera. Over time my looks would fade, my hairline recede, and my belt might loosen a few notches, but I could get by as long as I still had a thick twitching slab between my legs. There is always a market for hard cock. Fucking on camera allowed me to escape my problems. I was living a fantasy, the envy of most men.

Once the scenes ended and everyone went their separate ways, I'd return to my empty life and impatiently wait to do it all over again, hungry for another fix. The truth is, I was just a pawn built for sacrifice. Every contract I signed was for life rights, selling my soul for a buyout fee. My scenes will circulate online and continue to generate revenue for distributors long after I die. Porn is a cold machine, and I was at its mercy, a meat puppet set to expire.

At home, I ran myself a bath and sat in the tub as the water rose. I held my breath and slid down the enamel, sinking beneath the surface. I thought about the past, my childhood. Back to the beginning. Ten-year-old me snooping through my brother's bedroom, eyeing the crimson-painted trunk in front of his television. He called it "The Boo Box" to scare me away, but the fear only made me grow more curious. Home alone, I opened the Boo Box and pored over the stacks of video-game cartridges, CDs, and cassettes. An unmarked VHS tape tucked at the very bottom caught my eye—what secrets could it hold? I put it into the VCR and pressed play, staring wide-eyed as the picture faded in and revealed the title: *The X-rated Adventures of Peeping Tom*. Bronze bodies, wet lips, bouncing tits, and hard dicks. I didn't have a clue what I was watching but I liked the way it made me feel. Innocence lost. My childhood was over. From that point on, the only thing I ever thought about was porn. Kids my age looked up to celebrities like Michael Jordan and Leonardo DiCaprio. My idols were Peter North and Lexington Steele. I had one wish: to get in front of the camera. Against the odds, I chased the dream and made it real. I was a porn star. I got what I had always wanted, and it only brought me here.

Out of air, I raised my head above the water, then drained the tub. Wrapped in a towel, I sat at the desk in my living room and used my circumstance as motivation to write. About what, I didn't know, didn't care; anything to keep my mind occupied and to feel a sense of productivity. I purged onto the page, writing until my hands cramped and my eyes bled. Vivid, scattered memories of a fractured life. Little victories and nightmares. The past, present, and future; all roads seemingly leading to the same place: a farewell.

To whom it may concern,

> *I am of the belief that we, as performers, leave a small piece of ourselves behind on every set, but I'm afraid I've left too much over the years, losing who I was along the way. Now it's time for me to reclaim what's missing. I devoted myself to the business for as long as I*

could, but I think I'm ready to move on, to find my truth and start living it, whatever it might be.

I always knew that sooner or later all of this would have to come to an end. I've been living on borrowed time, scraping by while hoping everything would somehow fall into place, and I'd wake up a somebody. The dream has faded, passed me by while I was busy jacking off and burning bridges.

Bottom line: my heart is no longer in this, and therefore, neither is my dick. My journey has come to an end; it is time for this chapter to close and for another to begin. Onward and upward. Alert the media, it's official: Logan Pierce is retiring.

In the morning I got my test results: negative. I was spared. For now, at least. Someone somewhere was watching over me. Still, the moratorium continued. There were more first generations to be tested, and then if any of them were positive, all their first generations had to be tested, etc.

I called Beverly and told her the news.

"Congratulations," she said. "You popped your cherry."

"Yeah, how's that?"

"You work in this business long enough and you'll live through at least one HIV scare. Happens to everyone. Welcome to the club. You should celebrate."

"I don't really feel like partying right now."

"So don't celebrate. But know you've earned it. Let's focus on what's important then, getting you back to work and making some money once all this crap blows over."

"Yeah, I uh...I don't know, Bev."

"What's the matter, sweetie? Got cold feet all of a sudden?"

"I've been thinking. Maybe I don't want to do this anymore. This thing scared me."

"As it should. This is serious stuff. But chances are this whole mess was just a false-positive. It happens, and that's why we test the way we do, so all this stuff can be snuffed out early before it ever becomes a problem. And thinking's good, it means you're human and you actually care. Look, we still have a couple days before we're back in business so why don't you unplug, clear your head, and sleep on it? Whatever you're feeling now will pass, I promise."

"Yeah, maybe you're right."

"You didn't win *Best Male Newcomer* by accident. Trust me, this isn't the end. You belong here, sweetie."

"Thanks, Bev."

She hung up. I paced around the apartment. *You belong here.* I wondered what she meant by that. Was I here to do great things? To make a difference in the industry? Or did she mean I belong here in the biblical sense of reaping what I sow, and that accepting my fate would make the inevitable descent more sufferable?

I doubt she considered any of that and was just trying to placate me. Beverly had always been good to me, and in turn I tried to be the best client I could for her, herpes outbreaks and moral dilemmas notwithstanding. We were business partners, but we weren't friends. When it really came down to it, I was little more to her than a cheque at the end of the month. If I didn't work, she didn't get paid, and our relationship became moot. I understand that it's in a porn agent's nature to talk down an HIV scare in order to keep their clients amenable. I can't fault her for doing her job. It's all in the game.

But maybe she did have a point. I was too mixed up in everything, holding on too tight. It'd do me good to get out of LA and recharge, take advantage of this supposed freedom I had. Money was always scarce so what difference would it make if I treated myself to a little getaway? I rented a bungalow for a night in Joshua Tree.

I drove nearly four hours to the park entrance, heading in a few miles before I pulled off to the shoulder and parked. I walked toward a massive stack of boulders and scaled them, perching myself at the very top where I had a panoramic view of the desert solitude. Over 1200 square miles of undulating rock and top-heavy Yuccas with razor sharp spines and twisted limbs outstretched like hands reaching toward God. Wide blue skies allowed the sun to sear my skin. Warm gusts of wind whipped through my clothes and across my face. Other travellers occasionally drove by, their passing cars cut through the silence like crashing waves.

I stood up and walked to the edge, my toes overhanging. I concentrated my anger, my worries, and my self-doubt into a little ball, bottling it all in the back of my throat. I screamed as loudly as I could, releasing my pain into the ether, my voice echoing until it cracked, and the world fell quiet once again. I'm not sure what I accomplished, but I felt better, for the moment at least. Everyone deserves a good scream once in a while.

That night I sat under a glittering dome of stars, the constellations Taurus and Orion looking down from above. I thought about my letter. When this job was good it felt like a permanent vacation. Hot sex, fast cash, and no rules. Everything packaged together with the guarantee of internet fame. But when it was bad, I was dead broke with little hope. Even if I were to cut ties right now and walk away, my problems wouldn't stop just because I didn't fuck on camera anymore. Rent was still due at the first of the month.

After wrestling with myself, I chose to file the letter away for another time: I wasn't ready to leave. I had been in the business so long I had forgotten what life was like outside of the porn bubble. Maybe I was being a coward, scared at the thought of returning to a normal and otherwise *average* life. And maybe that's what I was always afraid of—being average. I was already of average looks, average intelligence, average suburban upbringing. Porn made me interesting. It gave me an identity. I might've only been a stunt cock, but at least I was in the movie.

By keeping the letter in the drawer, I was giving myself time to come up with an exit strategy. I was going to keep my head down and focus on earning. And when I would decide to call it quits, I wouldn't be at my lowest. I'd leave on my own terms, go out on top. All I had to do now was save my money and keep out of trouble—how hard could that be?

Three days later, testing concluded with no more positive results. The hold was lifted, and production resumed. Like all the other good boys and girls of porn, I put on a happy face and got busy.

SEVENTEEN

I usually planned trips home for the holidays as it's the one time of year I would see my family, but I decided to stay in town and pick up as many gigs as I could. Hollywood may take winter breaks, but porn never sleeps. Christmas morning was 75 degrees. With Bernie and Lou out of town, I spent the day alone at the beach. New Year's came and went.

I was back at Dirty Frank's, filling out my paperwork in the kitchen while my co-star sat next to me in makeup. Vic Malice was shooting the scene before ours on the sagging couch in the living room. Sex moans echoed through the house. My phone vibrated in my pocket. It was Sal Shooter. I took the call and slipped out through the sliding glass door to the backyard—a dirt lawn enclosed by a chain link fence.

"Yo, brother," said Sal. "What do ya say? How do ya feel? Tomorrow's the big day. The video drops first thing in the morning."

"Nice!" I said. "How do you think it turned out?"

"It's a fucking work of art, my friend. You're gonna love it, and so will the fans. This thing's gonna blow up."

"Oh, fuck yea."

"One small change though. The bosses went with a different angle for the title. It's now called, "Male Porn Star Struggles to Find Love.""

I didn't respond. Hearing the words made me cringe. It's not bad enough I had to contend with wood troubles, HIV scares, and herpes outbreaks. Now I was going to start the new year known as the loveless porn star.

"You still there?" he asked.

"Please tell me you're joking?"

"You don't like it?"

"Porn Star struggles to find love?" I said. "I didn't know we were shooting a dating ad, Sal. That title sounds like my whole life is me whining about being single when I'm paid to fuck for a living. Like I'm crying crocodile tears or something."

"Look man, I know, I know," he said. "But this is over my head. Trust me, you're gonna love the actual video. You know this website; they just want something that grabs people's attention."

"They want click-bait."

"...That, and something maybe a bit more relatable to the average viewer."

"You saying I'm not relatable?"

"Bro, not at all. I think you're a great dude and that shows in the video. All I'm saying is, a good-looking guy living care-free, hiking and hitting the beach everyday while banging hot chicks, isn't exactly the most universal lifestyle. That's the surface appeal of the video, sure, but the real hook is the struggle to maintain a relationship no matter who you are or what job you have. And by the end of the video, we have the viewers saying—"

"Porn stars are just like us," I said.

"Exactly. But look, I can call my bosses back and, you know, push for something different."

"No, no, it's fine," I said. "I get your point. It's just a title, right?"

"A hundred percent, bro. It's what gets the click on the video, but you're the reason why they'll stick around until the end."

"Fair enough. You sold me."

"So, we're cool?"

"Of course. Looking forward to the release."

"Bet-bet. I'll reach out tomorrow. Peace."

The video was live by the time I woke up the next morning, having already amassed nearly half a million views on the official YouTube page. The video also got picked up by *World Star Hip-Hop* and became the top trending video of the day, giving it another million hits. After watching it, I realized Sal was right. Even though the date was treated as the centerpiece, it was for a good reason. The inclusion of my dating life and lack of stable romantic relationships offered a touch of relatability, something the rest of the video was admittedly lacking, although I did look pretty cool scaling those cliffs and nailing my sex scene.

Comments on the video ranged from compliments about my body and candour, to people claiming I was a sociopath and a satanist. One person said my smile was so painfully annoying that if he were to ever see me on the street, he'd smash my teeth with a hammer. I guess that's why you're not supposed to read the comments. While I'd be happy to bask in showers of praise, thwarting expectations and stimulating new thought at the cost of making people slightly uncomfortable was fine by me. At least I knew I was doing something memorable.

Beyond the polarizing comments, I also received a small work offer. A website called *Totally Bro!* with a million Twitter followers reached out and asked if I'd write an essay about life in the biz—something provocative and loaded with sharp wit to get the readers laughing and turned on at the same time. I told them I'd think about it. Maybe it would open a new door and be a first step away from porn. Maybe it'd put me in the running for a full-time writing position with my own column: Lifestyles of the Hung and Horny, Between the Sheets with Logan Pierce. Maybe I'd even land a book deal—a bestseller with twenty weeks and counting on the New York Times' list with translations in five languages. Maybe I could humanize the porn star experience, after all.

Or maybe I was getting ahead of myself. First write the essay, then start a revolution.

EIGHTEEN

It was the third week of January. Awards season. AVN posted the nominees list in a press release on Twitter. I didn't bother to read it, it was always the same names up for the same awards. I had little reason to attend the expo outside of getting drunk and schmoozing, but Bernie and Lou convinced me to go by volunteering to be my entourage. They were practically foaming at the mouth at the thought of meeting their favourite starlets and partying with the rest of the circus.

In the past, I had seen people sneak civilians into the event, running around frantically, begging people to borrow their wristbands and I.D. badges so their friends could walk around unbothered without having to pay the hundred-dollar ticket fee. I wanted to avoid the hassle, so I emailed the organizers and told them that due to the success of my Pinnacle News documentary, another team wanted to follow me around and capture life at the expo. I said they'd need all access passes. AVN was only too eager to oblige.

The Hard Rock Hotel was the official home of AVN weekend. We arrived Saturday morning and strolled through the casino floor, past the slot machines and the sports betting lounge, deeper into the bowels past John Varvatos and Pink Taco. We reached the AVN registration booth and were presented with our ID badges and all-access wristbands. After a round of drinks at the Circle Bar, we flashed our credentials and breezed through security. I led the guys around the convention floor, manoeuvring between merchandise tables and tents, snaking through a barrage of porno enthusiasts and connoisseurs.

"Jesus," said Bernie. "It's like *Day of the Locust* in here."

We stuck our fingers inside display Fleshlights, were encouraged to grope uncanny life-sized sex dolls, and witnessed models being hogtied and whipped. We even saw Pauly Shore milling about. He had his own crowd of fans, his security detail trailing close behind.

At the Paragon Models booth, half-naked women stood in front of oversized posters of themselves, signing autographs and posing for photos with fans. Beverly was there in a sleek pantsuit, looking expensive. She had two iPhones sandwiched in one hand and a cocktail in the other.

"Hello, boys," she said. "Enjoying the view?"

"Loving it," said Lou, ogling the models.

"We aim to please," she said. Then noticing Bernie's wide grin. "And who is this stud?"

"Hi, I'm Bernie," he said, cheeks rosy.

"You certainly are," she said, sizing him up. "Is this the new boy on the block, Logan?"

"Hands off this one," I said. "He's *mainstream*."

"Heartbreaking," she said. "Well, if you ever decide to come over to the dark side, you know who to call."

"Oh, thank you, Mrs.—"

"*Miss*. La Bianca."

"Thank you, Miss La Bianca."

She turned to me. "He's precious. So, how are you? Excited for the show?"

"Excited to endure $14 beers and incoherent speeches?"

"Such a grump," she said. "At least you're nominated, right?"

"I'm *what?*"

"Did you not read the list? You're nominated, sweetie."

"What for?"

"*Unsung Swordsman.*"

"Get the fuck out of here."

"What's that?" asked Bernie.

"Most underrated cock," I said.

"He's being modest," said Beverly. "You wouldn't guess it just by looking at him, but your friend here can really fuck like a champ."

"Awe, thanks, Bev," I said. "You're too kind."

"A little ball busting never hurt anybody," she said, smiling at Bernie. She motioned across the floor with her iPhones. "Speaking of ball buster..."

I followed her gaze and spotted Milo Magnus standing at the Malibu Models booth, a maroon t-shirt tucked into his pleated trousers, chunky chrome around his wrist and neck. His bald head was shiny as ever. I stared until he made eye contact, then gave him a shit-eating grin. He remained sour-faced.

I rounded up the guys. "We're gonna keep doing the rounds. Catch you later, Bev."

"See you at the ceremony, sweetie," she said. "It was nice meeting you, boys. Especially you, Bernie."

"Dude," Bernie said, leaning into me. "I think your agent wants to fuck me."

"Oh yeah?" I said. "What gave it away?"

We continued wandering, collecting swag in the form of lube, condoms, and mini dildos modelled after dragon tails and octopus tentacles. Lou was on a mission to get a picture with his dream girl, Tori Black. She had just announced her official cum-back. We found her booth. The line to meet her stretched to eternity. Lou was committed, and I didn't dare rob the boy of his fantasy, so we took our place.

As we waited, someone brushed past. Raven haired. Statuesque. Clad in skintight PVC. It was Venus. She wasn't in prison, after all. Maybe she was on the run, hiding in plain sight.

"Gimme a minute," I said to the guys. Venus strutted off, and I made a beeline toward her, unsure of exactly what to say but sure

I had to say something. I called out her name as she rounded a corner.

She turned her attention, towering over me in platform stilettos. "Yes?"

"Holy shit," I said, giving her a once over. "I can't believe you're here. It's me, Logan."

"Logan?" she asked, not a shred of recognition in her eyes. "I'm sorry, have we met?"

"You know me. I'm a performer. We used to chat on Skype."

"One of my webcam worms, are you? Yes, hi, it's me, your goddess. If you want a picture, it's twenty bucks."

"I don't want a picture."

"Well, I don't chat for free. I have people waiting."

"Venus," I said, waving my hand in front of her. "It's Logan Pierce, hello? Don't you remember the last time we talked?"

"Spare me," she said, turning to walk away. "I don't have time for this."

"Hold on," I said, grabbing her arm.

"Excuse you," she said, shaking loose.

"Just tell me I'm not crazy."

"Logan—"

"I know what I saw."

"Oh really? What did you see?"

"Your bruised face, the rag over your eyes." I lowered my voice. "The *guy* on the floor?"

"And this means what to you? What have you done about it?"

I hesitated.

"Exactly. Do yourself a favour and forget about me. Turn around and walk away."

"Venus—"

"Enough!" she yelled, nearby heads turning. She leaned in and stared, her eyes smokey. "This conversation is over. Don't contact me again." She walked off, her heels clacking until the convention noise drowned them out. I looked around for leering eyes. Most were too fixated on all the abundant T&A to care.

I was stunned, more confused than ever. I was obviously poking around where I didn't belong. I wondered if the truth would satisfy me or just increase the itch of curiosity? Did I think Venus really killed someone? Did I care? No. She was right. I didn't go to the police. I didn't seek justice. I hadn't even told my friends. Venus and the body had already faded away, becoming just another footnote in a life filled with uncertainties and loose ends.

I wandered back, finding the guys had moved a whole five feet.

"Where'd you go?" said Lou.

"Catching up with an old friend."

Soon enough we made it to the front of the line. Lou got a signed 8x10 of Tori Black, and I did a piss poor job of convincing her that I was a male performer. Realizing we'd had enough of the expo, we bailed to get tacos and margaritas.

"And this is where I leave you, gentlemen," I said, finishing my drink.

"Go get 'em, stud," said Bernie.

"Bring home the gold," said Lou.

I went back to our room and changed into my suit and tie. It was time for the red carpet, an event I had been actively dreading. It wasn't the red carpet itself that bothered me. What bothered me was the pre-red carpet which extended all the way through the Hard Rock casino floor and out through a side entrance where we all huddled around, waiting to be let inside. Religious zealots stood on the corner and shouted at us, waving signs that read, "Sinners Rot," and "God Hates You." They protested every year but they're banned from the casinos, so their only option was to harass us from the parking lot.

Once inside, attendees slowly walked along a roped off path while fans, gamblers, and random hotel guests gawked at us and took photos that we'd never see and didn't really want taken in the first place. I smiled through gritted teeth, counting the minutes until it was over. Soon I walked the official red carpet, cycling through predetermined marks and plastering on a smile for all the industry photographers.

I bought a $14 beer, took my seat, and the ceremony began. The comedian host started off with a few jokes about STDs and abortion, followed by two A-list female performers who stumbled through their teleprompter banter before introducing the first category of nominees. Later, an off-brand rapper performed. Swarms of women rushed the stage, dancing and twerking, all competing for the spotlight.

An in-memoriam segment was dedicated to Aubrey Starflower. For a moment the audience sat in quiet, solemn reflection. Another young life lost, a shining star that burned too bright.

My category approached. I considered the possibilities of what might happen if my name were called. Would it mean I had been wrong for feeling like an outcast? That by accepting the lower rates I was, in fact, proving I was a team player? That any perceived slights had been exaggerated in my mind and I was actually well regarded in the business? I didn't have a speech prepared. I'd feel like a hypocrite taking the prize and expressing my unyielding gratitude for being given yet another novelty statue, publicly lauding the powers that be while flipping them the bird behind closed doors. I could be honest with the crowd and thank them for the recognition while sharing my dissatisfaction with the current state of affairs. I could talk about an industry that was as flawed as it was alluring, about the fact that improvement was possible but the work required to make it better for everyone would be never-ending. I could say that we were worth much more than the heft of our tits and the girth of our dicks, that greatness could be achieved only if we united with the shared goal of changing the industry for the better. Of course, I could just offer a simple thank you and leave it at that.

The presenter took the stage and spoke into the microphone.

"Here are the nominees for *Unsung Swordsman*."

One by one the names were announced, accompanied by R-rated highlight reels showcasing acting abilities and sweaty sex faces. Sporadic applause and cheers rose from the audience. When I saw myself appear I slid down in my seat, face hot and heart pounding, still without a clue of what to say if my name were called; so typical of me to remain indecisive until the last possible second.

The highlights ended and the presenter continued. "The winner of this year's *Unsung Swordsman* award is...Chad Savage!"

I let out a sigh of relief and mild disappointment. For a second there, I thought I had it. At least now I could relax. I clapped with everyone else as Chad took the stage, offering thanks to AVN and his agent. He disappeared behind the velvet curtains, and the next category was announced.

The show dragged on, becoming the familiar slideshow of years past: an unseen announcer rattling off lesser awards in rapid succession until most of the attendees left the ballroom and only empty chairs and discarded programs remained.

I ambled back to the casino floor and got a booth at the Hard Rock diner, ordering an apple pie with a slice of melted cheddar on top. The guys appeared, flush from the craps table.

"There he is," said Bernie.

"Hey superstar," said Lou. He patted Bernie's shoulder. "This guy just won three-hundred bucks, you believe that?"

"At least one of us is a winner," I said.

"Tough break, huh?" said Lou.

"What can you do?" I said. "I know it doesn't really mean anything, but it still would've been cool, you know?"

"Don't even worry about it," said Bernie. "Drinks are on me tonight."

"That's cause to celebrate."

"Remember the mantra," he said. "It's only French fries."

"That sounds good right about now," said Lou. "Let's get some grub for the table."

Just then Beverly approached in her glittering evening gown, diamonds on her neck. "Hello, boys," she said. "How are we?"

"What's up, Bev?" I said.

"You know it's all politics with these awards," she said. "If it's any consolation, you got the biggest applause out of everyone."

"You think so?"

"Without question. We'll get 'em next year, sweetie. I hope this isn't the end of the night for you boys. We have an afterparty going at the Cosmo."

"Now *that's* cause to celebrate," said Lou.

"Pay your tab," she said. "You can roll with me."

The four of us took a car to the Cosmo and made our way up to the 65th floor. "It's an open bar," said Beverly, as we stepped off the elevator and walked down the hall. "And, if any of you are in a skiing mood, a little bird told me there's plenty of powder." We came to a stop out front of the suite. She opened the double doors. "Welcome to Pornoland."

Music thumping, cameras flashing. Mini-skirts and highheels twirling on stripper poles and dancing on glass tabletops. Champagne flowed from every direction. All of it cast in the seedy glow of red neon. This was the Vegas I had promised the guys, something I knew they wouldn't soon forget.

Don Keedic was there and spotted me from across the room. "Hey, Pierce," he said, his eyes hidden behind aviators. "Bummer about the award, but if it were up to me, you would've gotten my vote."

"I appreciate that."

"Glad I found you. I saw your documentary thing. Good stuff, man, really dug it."

"Thanks. Yeah, it didn't turn out half bad."

"It got me thinking. I got a project I'm working on. Well, it's a series of projects I'm producing, edgy narrative driven stuff. I think you'd be a good fit for it. You're a solid performer and now that I know you like to write, I'm thinking maybe we could collaborate on some things. Who knows, with some experience behind the camera, you could become a triple threat, my friend." I wanted to play it cool, but my body betrayed me. My toothy grin reflected in his sunglasses. He knew he had me. "You like the sound of that?"

"Sure do."

"Good," he said. "Mull it over. We'll talk again back in town. Tonight, let's party!"

And party we did. Some drinks, some dancing, and a few trips down the slopes. At one point, Beverly and Bernie disappeared into one of the bedrooms. God only knows what happened behind that door. Later, I made out with two women on a balcony overlooking the strip, the lights of the city fusing into one. Everything after that was a blur.

We stirred in our room twenty minutes before check-out. A joint and some coffee brought us back to life. The Hard Rock crew was already tearing down banners and billboards, sanitizing the rooms, and bleaching the sheets before setting up for the next event.

We loaded the car and hit the road. The GPS estimated five hours to get us back. It was a long way home with a hangover, but at least it gave me time to think while the guys dozed. I might have left AVN empty handed, but I felt like I came away from the weekend with a renewed sense of purpose. Maybe moving behind the camera would be good for me, a natural evolution of my career. Or maybe I'd just be digging myself deeper into the hole. Sobering images of the longtime directors I'd encountered flashed in my mind—Vic Malice underpaying talent and subjecting them to the grimiest of shooting locations, Phil Holes sitting alone in his Hollywood condo, his eyes glazed as he edited scenes he had shot in that very room just hours earlier, a whiskey by his side, his further ambitions on permanent vacation. I wondered if I was destined to become like them if I continued on this path, if a life in porn had a fixed trajectory toward disappointment and regret. No. I refused to believe that. Their outcomes had no bearing on mine. I would create my own path, carve my own way. I knew how it was to be on the receiving end of the cameras, I could use that experience to create an ideal set. No more bottom dollar rates, no more male performers treated like extras, and no more dirty fucking floors. This was a chance to make a change. Sure, right now it was little more than a vague notion, but with some determination I knew I could make something of it.

I felt a peaceful stillness. No worries of the past or fears of the future. For the first time in a while, I was hopeful about things moving forward. I wanted to hold onto that feeling for as long as I could, to live with it forever.

But, for now, the month was nearly over. February loomed in the distance, and rent would soon be due. The machine was calling. It was time to get back to work.

Acknowledgements

Mom and Dad for the endless support. Ryan and Kim at Orbis Tertius Press for taking a chance. Johnny White for the photos. Elle Nash for everything. Rob H. for the hard truths. Eva, Dan H., Ruth, JD, Cait, and Jess for peer reviewing. Ryan C. for the inspiration. Mina for the pitch notes. My writing partner, Baby, for only occasionally demanding attention. The porn industry for giving me a place to grow. The city of Los Angeles for being my second home. The city of Philadelphia for keeping me in check.

GO BIRDS!

www.ingramcontent.com/pod-product-compliance
Lightning Source LLC
Chambersburg PA
CBHW031437270326
41930CB00007B/748